Mid Pines Country Club
Pine Needles Country Club

Officers of the Club

Kelly R. Miller	*President*
Bonnie Bell McGowan	*Vice-President*
John M. May	*Secretary-Treasurer*

Directors

Peggy Kirk Bell   W. Kirk Bell   Jack Campbell

James Marsh   Bonnie Bell McGowan   Pat McGowan

Kelly R. Miller   Peggy Bell Miller   Preston Ridenhour Young

Founding Members

Joe Agresta & Jo Ann Williams
Tony & Mary Catherine Austin
Brent & Dede Bailey
Casey Bierer
Bob & Janet Carl
Murray & Mary Lynne Clark
Jim & Wendy Dodson
Jim & Pam Dougherty
Gary DeShazer
Jim & Shelby Faircloth
Mike & Bea Fields
Bill & D.Ann Hanna
Buck & Marianne Kernan

Chris & Amy Knott
Chris Larsen
Emmet & Mary Logan
Scott & Molly Mahoney
Keith & Camie Marion
Noel & Jamie McDevitt
Jay Mickle
Rob & Patricia Robbins
Richard Schmidt
Bill & Cathy Smith
Tom & Ilana Stewart
Clement & Barbara Williams

Mid Pines Country Club
Pine Needles Country Club

Officers of the Club

Kelly R. Miller	President
Bonnie Bell McGowan	Vice-President
John M. May	Secretary-Treasurer

Directors

Peggy Kirk Bell   W. Kirk Bell   Jack Campbell

James Marsh   Bonnie Bell McGowan   Pat McGowan

Kelly R. Miller   Peggy Bell Miller   Preston Ridenhour Young

Founding Members

Joe Agresta & Jo Ann Williams
Tony & Mary Catherine Austin
Murray & Mary Lynne Clark
Jim & Wendy Dodson
Jim & Pam Dougherty
Mike & Bea Fields
Bill & D. Ann Hanna
Buck & Marianne Kernan

Chris & Amy Knott
Chris Larsen
Emmet & Mary Logan
Keith & Carnie Marlon
Jay Mickle
Rob & Patricia Robbins
Richard Schmidt
Bill & Cathy Smith
Clement & Barbara Williams

SANDHILLS CLASSICS

THE STORIES
OF MID PINES
AND PINE NEEDLES

BY LEE PACE
FOREWORDS BY DICK TAYLOR AND BILL FIELDS
AFTERWORD BY JAMES DODSON

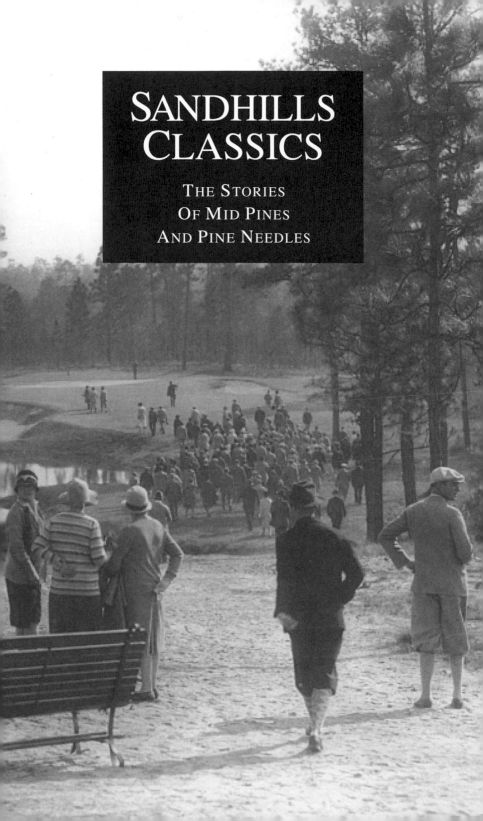

SANDHILLS CLASSICS

THE STORIES
OF MID PINES
AND PINE NEEDLES

SANDHILLS CLASSICS

THE STORIES OF PINE NEEDLES AND MID PINES

Published by Pine Needles Country Club Inc.
& Mid Pines Development Group LLC.

Library of Congress Catalog Card Number 96-067058
ISBN: 0-9651076-0-4
Book Design by Sue Pace

Printed in Canada

Front end sheet shows Donald Ross teeing off on the original
third hole (today the second) with the Pine Needles Inn in the
background (photo by John Hemmer); back end sheet shows an
aerial view of Mid Pines Inn during the mid-20th century
(photo from Mid Pines Inn & Golf Club).

ABOUT THE AUTHOR

Lee Pace is a Chapel Hill-based writer who has written
hundreds of thousands of words over two decades about
the Sandhills area golf experience. He has written about
Mid Pines and Pine Needles for *GOLF*, *Links* and
Pine Straw magazines, among others. He ghost-authored
with Peggy Kirk Bell her 2001 book, *The Gift of Golf*.

Dedicated to the memory of
Maisie and Frank Cosgrove and Warren Bell—
three people of unlimited vision, standards and energy
who helped make Mid Pines and Pine Needles
pleasant places to visit.

The original fourth hole at Pine Needles (shown on title page and above) is now the third hole and looks much like it did decades later when owners Bullet and Peggy Bell played the hole (right).

PINE NEEDLES LODGE & GOLF CLUB

CONTENTS

1. The Early Days at Knollwood
Page 18

2. The Cosgroves of Mid Pines
Page 38

3. The Bells of Pine Needles
Page 58

4. The Genius of Donald Ross
Page 82

5. The Teaching Tradition
Page 106

6. Peggy's Pearls: Tips for Better Golf
Page 114

7. The Modern Era
Page 124

8. Photo Album
Page 142

Gallery circles 18th green as women's tournament concludes in 1928.

PINE NEEDLES

BY DICK TAYLOR

This is a personal labor of love. It isn't even labor. When asked to provide the foreword to this book, this history of Pine Needles and the Bell family, it seemed an easy task. Write about old friends and the club where you spend all of your golfing time? Piece of cake.

But it wasn't and isn't, when it became apparent the impact "The Needles" and the Bells have had upon my life, and on golf. The true labor of love is embodied in the rebuilding of Pine Needles by Warren and Peggy Bell and the raising of diverse children who now, with spouses, are continuing the tradition of relaxed elegance at arguably the greatest small resort on the planet.

Picture a golf course used as a combat training site in World War II and Army barracks where men-only bunked at fifteen dollars per night, including meals and golf, and you can see what Warren and Peggy and the family have wrought over the years. Peggy gives total credit for this fruition to her late husband, who was driven to bring about his dream and vision of the perfect resort.

"I was on a cloud," says Peggy, "while Bullet put this all together. He said I had no idea what it took and then to keep it that way, and he was right." But that has been the charm of this love story—the bright, critical, super-hyper successful husband and the distaff Will Rogers who never met a person she didn't like and helped thousands repair their golf swings and have more fun at the game.

In 1962 I was interviewed for the job of editor of *Golf World* magazine (which was published at the time in Southern Pines) and in the process of scouting the place dropped by Pine Needles, having met Peggy years ago. Her advice still rings: "Take the job! This is one of the best places in the world to live and raise kids. And you can play golf here." This became part of the equation in deciding to move from West Palm Beach, Florida, and it was one of the few great decisions I have made in my life.

Although it's a resort, I consider Pine Needles my home course, and the ever-growing Bell-McGowan-Miller family as family, too; sort of the in-laws you wish you had, and this has been a factor in my life. During my first ten years at *Golf World*, I was offered positions at the United States Golf Association, *GOLF* magazine and the National Golf Foundation. In the first two instances I made money the obstacle, but the third time around I told the truth. I did not want to leave the area and the good friends, the Bells being high on the list. When Charley Price, Bob Drum and Harvie Ward came to the area, I was replete with best friends. The second greatest decision was to stay put.

Warren Bell would give you a thoughtful answer to a thorny problem and usually was right. He is the only man I have known who had only black and white in his thinking, no shadings whatsoever, and considered hypocrisy and dishonesty mortal sins. Peggy Bell is more forgiving but still is surprised when she discovers someone is not on the up-and-up. She takes everyone at face value.

Annual patrons of Pine Needles come for three reasons—the golf, of course, and the uncrowded conditions, and the host family. At lunch they circulate among the guests, and Peggy is usually seen swinging an imaginary club, giving someone a tableside lesson.

Regulars have also watched the family grow up and have had the pleasure to feel as surrogate grandparents as the third generation at The Needles cavorted at lunchtime during the 1980s and '90s.

Not unlike a number of famous people, Peggy Kirk Bell doesn't know she is one of them and sputters when confronted with the word. People who think they are famous usually aren't. Warren and Peggy Bell have left an enduring legacy and you can sense it as you drive into the Pine Needles resort compound.

I first met Peggy Kirk in 1948. I was golf editor of the *Palm Beach Post* when she won the first of two Palm Beach Women's Amateur championships at The Breakers. She was a regular on the winter Grapefruit Circuit, played by a band of golf-loving gals who started in Miami and moved to Hollywood, Palm Beach, Sebring, St. Augustine and then up to Pinehurst. There was no professional tour. She became famed during the

1940s when she won the Titleholders in Augusta, the ladies' equivalent of the Masters that included all the professionals then playing. She also won the North and South Amateur in Pinehurst, the Eastern and the International Four-Ball with Babe Zaharias. "Babe told me to relax, she'd take care of winning," Peggy recalls, and the Babe did.

At the Babe's urging, she turned pro in 1950, and despite the closely-knit group of more established professionals who claim LPGA founder status, she was also a founder and has a membership card from the first-president Babe to prove it.

Peggy was born in 1921 in Findlay, Ohio, the daughter of Robert and Grace Kirk. At Findlay High School, she was female athlete of the year three successive years, with basketball and baseball her strong suits. She began golf following high school.

At the same time Warren Bell, who would become her husband in 1953, was one of the most widely recruited basketball point

Peggy and Bullet look at plans for growing their resort before Peg takes off for another venture onto the LPGA Tour.

guards of his time, opting for Ohio State. The childhood sweethearts had not continued their "romance" past the third grade. Peg says she had a crush on him in high school, but "he was as cocky as they come and he had a girlfriend."

College and World War II occupied both and it wasn't until 1953 that the rekindled romance culminated in marriage. By then "Bullet" Bell, named for his speed as a swimmer, had played pro basketball for the Fort Wayne Pistons (now Detroit) and had been Spalding's ace salesman. They decided their future was in building their own golf club.

Peggy was not without means, as her father had built upon a four-city wholesale grocery business by adding real estate of all types to his portfolio. He gave his children income property after they left high school, "to see how we would handle it," says Peggy, and once she had her first spree and could not pay her own taxes, she learned how to handle money.

She and Bullet put $20,000 into the kitty and friends "Pop" and Maisie Cosgrove and Julius Boros, their son-in-law, added $30,000 to purchase Pine Needles in 1953 from the Catholic Diocese of Raleigh, which had bought the property from George Dunlap five years earlier. Two years later, the Bells bought their partners out for $60,000, the amount needed by the Cosgroves to buy Mid Pines. The Cosgroves had been leasing that resort.

In 1994, the Bell family and investment partners purchased Mid Pines from a hotel chain and quickly brought the charming resort up to speed, particularly the golf course, also a Donald Ross design. Julius and brother Ernie Boros ran the golf operation in the 1950s and '60s, and Pinehurst still felt like home to Julius years after he had departed for Florida. Encountering him on tour, he would invariably ask, "How are things back home?" And the latest happenings would be relayed. Guests at both resorts may opt to play either of the two courses, if tee times are available, by walking across the street.

Looking around today, the $50,000 the Bells and partners paid at first might seem a great bargain, but as has been said, all they got was a golf course, albeit a great one, and an Army barracks; they were practically starting from scratch.

But year by year, this labor of love continued to grow into one of the class resorts anywhere, and it is unabated. The latest adjunct is the Learning Center at the far end of the practice range, a state-of-the-art star-tech building for the seriously ailing golf swing as well as for a little tweak and tightening of a very good swing. You'll find son-in-law Pat McGowan on these acres happily giving lessons alongside "Ma" Bell. Other family members are active as well. Son-in-law Kelly Miller is general manager, and Bonnie Bell McGowan, Peggy Ann Miller and Kirk Bell have all pitched in at various points in their lives, from working the front desk to teaching in the golf schools.

Warren Bell would have been a huge success at whatever endeavor he chose. Peggy Bell was destined to be an influence in the growth of golf in America. Among her many honors is the USGA Bobby Jones Sportsmanship Award. "I was shocked when I got it and I still don't know why," says Peggy to this day.

Speaking for the large panel of golf supporters who voted for her, it was one way to say thank you for her unselfishness to the game and the people in it, including a lot of struggling youngsters, and to tell her we love her for being who and what she is and what she means to this game we all love. ∎

Dick Taylor was a writer and editor for "Golfworld" from 1965-89 and later contributed to "Senior Golf," "Golfweek," and "Links" magazines. He died at his Pinehurst home in 1997.

The year 1952 was a big one for golfers with North Carolina ties, as Julius Boros (U.S. Open), Harvie Ward (British Amateur), Johnny Palmer (Canadian Open) and Dick Chapman (French Amateur) collected significant victories. Their accomplishments were recognized at a celebratory tournament at Mid Pines in November 1952, with Sam Snead (dark shirt and hat in center of green) winning the event.

MID PINES

BY BILL FIELDS

S everal years ago, I was driving through Yellowstone National Park in the early morning when I pulled over to take a photograph. The scene was so still and quiet that I could remember only one other place I had been that matched its serenity. That would have been out on the fairways at Mid Pines, on any number of countless evenings in the 1970s, when it was just me, my clubs, the ball and my dreams.

There are longer courses, tougher courses, better courses. But to me, there is no more special course than Mid Pines. Some of the shots I see still: the tee shot on the short second hole, when the hole is tucked in the right corner of the green; the decision at the fourth—lay up or try to get close off the tee; the approach to the elf-sized green at number nine; the matter of which fairway wood to play to the par-three thirteenth; the difficult drive off the elevated tee at the sixteenth. And how about standing in the eighteenth fairway with a six-iron in your hand, needing to get your ball up the rise and hold it on the green, that grand old hotel looming in the background?

History will remember the 1970s as a decade of crises of energy, hostages, government, fashion—but for me it was mostly about golf, largely played at Mid Pines.

I got my first taste of the place as a kid, thanks to the kindness of a neighbor, Dom Scali, who presided over the Mid Pines locker room and gladly let me tag along with his children and play the course when things were slow. He was also responsible for procuring the odd con-

MID PINES INN & GOLF CLUB

One of the nicest sights in golf–the approach to the 18th at Mid Pines.

vention leftover for me, which explains why I was the only student at Southern Pines Middle School who wore an Amana cap.

Jim Boros, nephew of Julius, was the head professional at Mid Pines by the time I was in high school, and he let me work after school and in the summer cleaning clubs, parking golf carts and picking up practice balls on the property's truncated range. Coming as it did after I had decided to leave my first job, preparing fried seafood plates at a nearby restaurant, this one offered many advantages, not the least of which was that I didn't smell like flounder and hushpuppies when I got home. At Mid Pines, my tastes shifted to the steamed hot dogs with mustard and relish that Cynthia sold at the tenth-tee snack stand. Jim was a solid enough player himself in those years, and he was eager enough to help a kid with a dream, but there was one thing he couldn't tolerate. A shank. Not hitting one, but merely observing one. I hit a semi-lateral playing with him once and I can still see the look on his face.

After my dream of playing golf for a living gave way to the reality that I would not, Mid Pines helped pay for college when I worked as a bellman there during the summers home from my freshman and sophomore years in Chapel Hill. Climbing three flights with suitcases got me in great shape, and the money came in handy.

Those tips are long gone, but you can't spend memories, and Mid Pines gave me plenty. ■

Southern Pines native Bill Fields is a senior editor with "Golf World" magazine in Wilton, Connecticut.

CHAPTER ONE

THE EARLY DAYS AT KNOLLWOOD

R ichard Tufts walked out of the Ambassador Hotel late the night of October 1st, 1931, onto 45th Street in New York City. The evening had been part fascination, part frustration. His host had been Eldridge R. Johnson, the inventor of the Victor Talking Machine and a frequent visitor to Pinehurst, the golf resort in the North Carolina Sandhills which the Tufts family owned and operated. Johnson was also a key investor along with the Tufts in a golf resort called Pine Needles Inn, located about four miles away in Southern Pines.

The Great Depression was choking the lifeblood out of families and businesses nationwide in the early 1930s, and Pinehurst Incorporated and its ancillary businesses, including Pine Needles Inn and its sister property across the street, Mid Pines Country Club, weren't spared the misery of red ink and foreclosures. When Pine Needles, a state-of-the-art, five-story hotel opened for business on January 28th, 1928, Johnson had invested $124,000 and Pinehurst Inc. $150,000 through purchase of stock; those funds, combined with a first mortgage from Virginia Trust Co. of $250,000 and sale of common stock to assorted other investors, provided the capital for the hotel and a golf course created by the famous Scottish golf designer, Donald Ross.

The timing couldn't have been worse.

It was only twenty-one months after the first tournament ever played at Pine Needles—a ladies open won by Virginia Van Wie in

Mid Pines (top) and Pine Needles joined Sandhills horizon in the 1920s as the Tufts family expanded its Pinehurst operations.

February, 1928—that Black Tuesday hit and launched the United States into the throes of the Depression. Pine Needles never showed a profit, and Pinehurst Inc. absorbed its operating losses and bought its first mortgage subrogated notes as they came due. Tufts, vice president of Pinehurst Inc., decided to appeal directly to Johnson for help in financing Pine Needles during the lean times. Without help, Tufts believed, Pine Needles would not survive.

Johnson served Tufts grouse imported from Scotland and entertained him with stories about the fragility of business enterprises. Most memorable to Tufts was an account of a skirmish with disaster early in the century by the Victor Talking Machine Company. A key ingredient in the manufacturing process for records was shellac, a commodity in short supply but still available in sufficient enough quantities for Victor's needs. But when the "Merry Widow" hat became popular shortly afterward, the price of shellac skyrocketed because of the high demand for the substance in making the stiff brims of the hat.

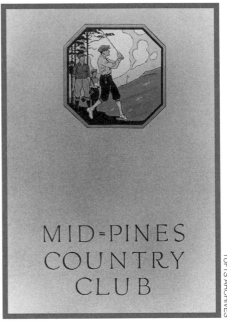

"If that hat had remained popular," Johnson told Tufts, "my business would have failed."

Despite the hospitality and engaging conversation, Johnson turned down Tufts' request for money. And as Tufts left that evening, he could see the end for Pine Needles.

A few steps down the sidewalk, he was approached by a beggar. Tufts turned him down in short order.

Then he stopped.

"I'm nothing more than a beggar myself," Tufts thought to himself. He gave the man five dollars.

"Maybe Mr. Johnson will decide to do the same for me," Tufts hoped.

***

Pinehurst was a vibrant, lively spot in golf and social circles in the late 1910s. The likes of Walter Hagen and Francis Ouimet were winning golf tournaments there. Annie Oakley was teaching at the gun club. The Rockefellers and du Ponts, the Morgans and Sousas were guests at the opulent Carolina Hotel. Sportsmen hunted quail and dove; the fairer sex perused the lavish cases of fashions from Paris, silks from Samarkand and rubies from from the rich mountains of Burma displayed in the hotel lobby.

Life moved at a slower pace, simply because it had to. Automobiles were luxuries, and train rides could be long and tedious. So travelers often stayed at their destinations for long periods. They ate leisurely meals, wrote lengthy letters, played word games that would seem silly today. Communication was by post, telegraph and newspaper—but only occasionally by that instrument that allowed you to speak to someone you couldn't see.

Pinehurst was located a seventeen-hour train ride from New York. In the late fall, winter and early spring, it was a convenient escape from the snow and biting winds of New York, Boston, Chicago and Detroit. The Carolina Hotel was turning away some 15,000 to 20,000 visitors a year in February and March. The other hostelries in the village were full as well—the Holly Inn, the Berkshire, the Pine Crest Inn, the Lexington and the Harvard.

But for some, the Carolina (later named the Pinehurst Hotel), and the village had become *too* lively—if you can believe that. "There is the desire of a number of old Pinehurst guests who want to have comfortable quarters where they can be away from the activities of the hotels," said Leonard Tufts, son of resort founder James Walker Tufts and the resort chief from James' death in 1902 until his own bad health forced his retirement in the mid-1930s.

For some time Tufts and a handful of area businessmen and regular visitors to Pinehurst had had their eyes on nearly six thousand acres of land between Pinehurst and Southern Pines known as Knollwood. There they envisioned a posh private club with golf and lodging and a surrounding residential community.

Thus was conceived Mid Pines Country Club.

The first official meeting of Mid Pines Country Club was held in January, 1921. James B. Barber of Pinehurst, founder of Barber Steamship Line Incorporated of New York, was elected president. Tufts was vice president and general manager. A.S. Newcomb, a real estate agent, was secretary/treasurer. Donald Ross, the golf architect,

Cars and a dirt driveway have changed over time outside Mid Pines.

was a founding member, as was L.M. Boomer, a partner with the du Pont family in owning the Waldorf-Astoria in New York City.

The club was incorporated with total authorized capital of $375,000, divided into one hundred and fifty shares to be sold for $2,500 each. (In the end, though, barely half of the shares would be sold; by April, 1928, Mid Pines had sold only seventy-one shares of stock, and twelve more were sold by 1933.) The stock offering was sponsored by Knollwood Incorporated, a company formed in 1920 by the Tufts to buy and develop the land between Southern Pines and Pinehurst. There were

MID PINES INN & GOLF CLUB

ten original stockholders in Mid Pines Country Club.

The offering was endorsed by men of ample connections, as one sales pitch emphasized in mentioning Tufts, Ross and Boomer as a "trio whose combined knowledge of what people desire in the way of housing and food and outdoor entertainment and how to get it is probably not equalled by any other group of several times its size in the world."

Architect Aymer Embury II of New York was chosen to design the club and lodgings. He envisioned a three-story Georgian style building, some five hundred feet from end to end, half with brick veneer and half with wood siding. One of the interesting tweakings of the design is still a conversation piece today—the assortment of owls, swans, serpents, boars, lions and other figures in relief on the ceiling of the room that now constitutes the inn's lounge.

Ross, who had already built four courses at Pinehurst Country Club, would design the original plan of thirty-six holes of golf (though only eighteen would be built). Ross had his choice of some five thousand acres and chose a site just below a ridge of hills that would provide protection from the wind.

The founders' intention was to make only enough profit to pay stockholders a dividend to cover their annual dues of $150. There were no advertising costs, musician costs or profits to worry about. With rates slightly lower than the Carolina (top rates at the Carolina in 1924 were $154 a week, compared to $119 at Mid Pines), members could pay for their dues and eventually the cost of their stock by staying at Mid Pines. One member was delighted to figure that in three weeks at Mid Pines, he saved enough over the room, board and golf costs at the Carolina Hotel to pay for his yearly dues and six percent interest on his $2,500 stock certificate.

The club purchased one hundred and eighty acres at $125 each. The golf course cost $46,152.15 to build, the hotel $262,929.78; the total bill was $456,699.15. The golf course opened in November, 1921, and the first tournament was held January 24th of the following year. Arthur Yates of Oak Hill Club in Rochester, New York, shot a seventy-nine to win that event. The hotel and clubhouse opened in late January, 1922.

By the fall of 1923 there were forty-six members, among them George T. Dunlap, partner in the world's largest publishing firm, Grosset & Dunlap; John Sprunt Hill, the well-known banker from Durham; Thomas E. Wilson, founder of Wilson Sporting Goods; Leonard Tufts and his three sons, James, Albert and Richard; Frank V. du Pont of Wilmington, Delaware; Frank Presbrey of New York, an advertising executive and key associate of the Tufts family; William N. Reynolds of Winston-Salem, patriarch of the wealthy tobacco family; and Donald Ross, the Scottish golf professional who'd become enamored of course design upon his arrival in Pinehurst late in 1900.

Management hoped that members and potential full-time residents would be drawn by the beauty and the country setting. Leonard Tufts was building a home valued at $100,000 in the early 1920s in Knollwood. Another resident was Judge W.A. Way of Pittsburgh.

Mid-Pines Country Club

Pinehurst, N. C.

DINNER

Grapefruit Maraschino

Vegetable Soup		Beef Bouillon
Queen Olives	Celery Hearts	Spiced Watermelon
Mustard Pickles		Pearl Onions

Cream of Wheat

Broiled Shad with Roe
Boiled Ox Tongue with Fresh Spinach
Fricassee of Chicken Orient
Baked Banana Glace

Roast Milk Fed Chicken Currant Jelly
Roast Leg of Veal Dish Gravy

Boiled and Mashed Potatoes   Steamed Sweet Potatoes
Boiled Onions   Stewed Corn
Steamed Rice

Lettuce Hearts   Peach Salad
French Mayonnaise Roquefort Dressing

Vienna Bread   Graham Bread

Baked Cracker Pudding Foam Sauce
Maple Walnut Sundae   Vanilla Ice Cream
Apple Pie   Assorted Cake

American Cheese   Cream Cheese   Roquefort Cheese
Toasted Saltines
Mixed Nuts   Dates   Apples   Oranges
Demi tasse

March 11, 1929

Leisurely dinners were a part of the Mid Pines experience in its early days. Over the years, spiced watermelon, boiled ox tongue and dates for dessert have gone the way of the sand putting green.

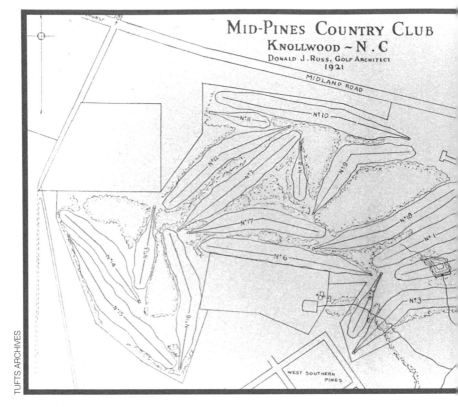

"It looked good to me when I saw this climate and this development of golf, hotels, conveniences for winter life, and particularly the short run from the North," Way said in deciding why he took an interest in the area. "Florida is twice as far away, and therefore it is twice as difficult to reach quickly. This is the most accessible place for a man from the east."

A 1923 advertisement predicted: "Knollwood Village will be the home of hundreds of golf enthusiasts and the most attractive village in North Carolina." Another ad later in the year noted that $60,000 had recently been spent on a new school in Southern Pines, $75,000 on one in Aberdeen and $60,000 on another in Pinehurst. The conclusion? "Expansion on a big scale is imperative in all directions immediately surrounding Knollwood."

Nonetheless, standards were high for invitations to join. "The stock is not to be offered promiscuously, but to a clientele that will ensure congeniality and good fellowship, which is the club's ideal," said a

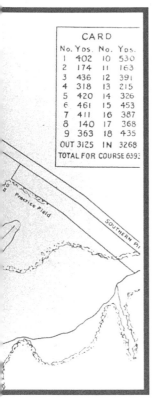

CARD			
No.	Yds.	No.	Yds.
1	402	10	530
2	174	11	163
3	436	12	391
4	318	13	215
5	420	14	326
6	461	15	453
7	411	16	387
8	140	17	368
9	363	18	435
OUT 3125		IN	3268
TOTAL FOR COURSE 6393			

1921 memo by Leonard Tufts, who stressed in another directive that Mid Pines wasn't to be a hell-raising retreat for bachelors: "We are much more interested in getting men with their wives, if desirable, than we are men alone."

Quite a discussion was carried on through the mails over the merits of selling stock to a certain whiskey manufacturer from Waterloo, Canada. "I know him slightly, but he is a pleasant man to meet and of good reputation in his home town," Ross wrote to Tufts. "He manufactures whiskey, but that is nothing against him, but some of the other members might think differently."

Another member, Calvert Crary, wrote: "While, personally, I do not like to associate with whiskey manufacturers, at the same time think that would hardly bar one from becoming a member of the Mid Pines Club if the applicant had the endorsement of some good men."

The man was Edward Seagram. You've heard the name. Apparently, he never joined the club.

Another potential member was skewered because of a nervous personality: "It might be well to consider his application pretty carefully for a nervous, high-strung man in a peaceful organization such as the Mid Pines Club might make it less pleasant for the other members," Tufts cautioned in another memo. Another member opined: "He has a rather pompous, conceited air about him which I did not like."

Business was good in the early days at Mid Pines. The room count rose from 1,887 in its inaugural 1921-22 season steadily to a high of 4,825 in 1928-29. The club posted an operating profit each of its first seven years, but interest payments on the bonds it sold to help finance the original construction left it with a net loss for the first five years. Finally, in its sixth year, the club posted a net profit of $41.09, and that figure rose to $1,249.96 in 1928-29. Room and board accounted for nearly all of the club's income, though the audit each year listed miscellaneous income from mineral water ($185.11 in 1927-28), the newsstand ($76.96), cigars ($102.29) and pork ($335.27). Presumably the pork sold at Mid Pines was homemade sausage from the pig farm on land beyond the No. 3 golf course at Pinehurst Country Club, suggests Tufts family descendant Peter Tufts of Seven Lakes.

While Mid Pines was doing a good business, its private nature could only help so much with alleviating overflow from the hotel and inns in Pinehurst. Plus, there were hundreds of potential homesites in Knollwood that had to be developed. Thus Pine Needles was created. A meeting was held at Jack's Grill in Southern Pines on January 22nd, 1926, and Henry Page, vice president of Page Trust Company of Aberdeen, outlined the plan to potential investors.

"It is a Sandhills business scheme handled and controlled by Sandhills businessmen and men who are known by everyone in the Sandhills," said an editorial in the January 29th, 1926, *Sandhills Citizen*. "When James Barber, Judge Way, Richard Tufts, Ralph Page, Henry Page and A.S. Newcomb come to you with a business proposition, it is a guarantee that the proposition is a good one."

The property was called "Pine Needle Inn" during the first month of its planning, then newspaper reports and advertisements added the plural "Pine Needles." A meeting of the new corporation's board of directors held in January, 1927, included a lively discussion of the name, with some feeling too much was made of the "pine" in the area, but others argued that the pine tree was becoming more and more an asset to the area. "The sentiment was the name has a good sound on the tongue," according to the *Citizen*.

Construction of the Pine Needles hotel and golf course began in early 1927. Architect Lyman Sise of Boston, an in-law of Leonard Tufts, was retained and soon unveiled drawings for an English Tudor style hotel that would sit atop a knoll and be visible for miles. (Sise's firm, Haven & Hoyt, was working on a new wing at the Holly Inn in Pinehurst at the same time.) No expense was spared to make it the finest in the South. The structure was fireproof and steel-framed. Each room had a bath and phone; some had parlors. More than $100,000 of North Carolina furniture was purchased. Intricate wood trim surrounded the doors and windows, and Chinese and Indian rugs were placed through the public rooms on the ground floor.

While purchase of a share of Mid Pines stock in the 1920s included club membership, Pine Needles was more of a real-estate driven enterprise. A share of preferred stock in it cost $3,000 and included one of the first fifty building lots staked out around the golf course. The land cost $170,000, the golf course and grounds $50,000, the hotel $390,000, quarters for staff and a power plant $40,000, and furnishings $100,000—for a total of three-quarters of a million dollars.

Diners at the new Pine Needles Inn enjoyed an ornate decor of intriguing crown moldings, hardwood floors and fine china.

Pine Needles was incorporated March 19th, 1927, and Richard Tufts was elected president of the new corporation. He predicted profits of $30,000 to $40,000 a year—sufficient to pay interest on the mortgage and preferred stock and help retire the mortgage. Sales of the remaining two hundred lots within a few years, Tufts believed, would further retire the indebtedness and be used for improvements to the hotel.

A fifteen-acre lake was created on the back nine by damming a stream that ran through the property. An early newspaper account said the eleventh hole (today the tenth) "will be among most difficult in the

Sandhills. The pond looks like a graveyard for many balls." A second course was planned, and the *Pinehurst Outlook* said, "There is little doubt that it will be required within a year or so."

The hotel opened on January 28th, 1928. The first golf event was held in early February, the First Annual Women's Mid-South Open Championship, with Virginia Van Wie defeating Glenna Collett on the fourth extra hole. Miss Collett, who later married Edwin Vare, lived at Pine Needles and sold real estate as she worked toward becoming the finest American woman golfer of the 1920s and '30s.

So from early 1928 until October, 1929, the Tufts and their associates had created two vibrant, active properties in Southern Pines and had successfully expanded their operations away from their hub in the village of Pinehurst.

The personalities for both Mid Pines and Pine Needles were then enhanced (and still are today) by their locations on Midland Road, a five-mile tunnel of towering longleaf pine trees stretching from Southern Pines to Pinehurst. At least one Sandhills real-estate agent takes any first-time visitor to the area on a leisurely drive from one end of Midland Road to the other. The newcomers inhale the fresh pine scent, marvel over the stately pines sitting in the median, see the blue skies harmonizing with the rich greens of the golf courses along the way—and often they're hooked.

Midland Road originally was the route of the Pinehurst Railroad Corporation's trolley line, constructed in 1895-96, which transported guests to the infant Pinehurst resort from the train depot in Southern Pines. A decade later, the trolley had been discontinued and Leonard Tufts offered in 1907 to build half the road if the town of Southern Pines paid for the rest.

Tufts completed his half of the road as scheduled, but Southern Pines ran out of money with a mile to go. So author and Southern Pines resident James Boyd contributed more than $1,000 to finance completion of the road. About all you say of this early road was that it was serviceable—if not easy to traverse. "The old sandy road was very uncomfortable, very tiresome and very unprogressive," an early 1910s issue of the *Outlook* said. As road-building technology improved over the years, the quality of the road improved.

Two lanes run in each direction and the median is covered with pine straw, shrubs and towering pines. There are few signs along the way, and those that exist are understated and generally harmonize with their surroundings. The sign at the entrance to Pine Needles, for in-

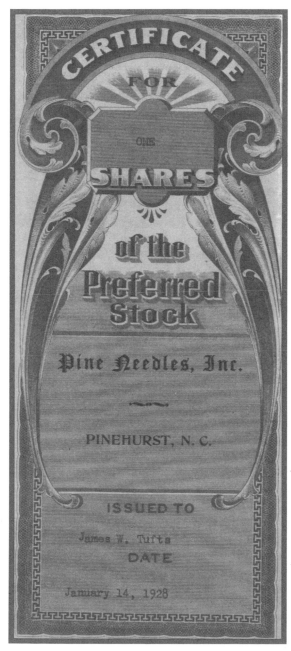

James Tufts
of Pinehurst
was issued
this share of
Pine Needles
stock in 1928
in return for
$3,000.

stance, features the resort's name and pine cone logo carved from dark wood. Across the road, the brick columns at the entrance to Mid Pines and its row of stand-alone cottages are painted white and adorned with bronze pineapples, the symbol of hospitality.

Mid Pines was nearing adolescence and Pine Needles was still an infant when the crash of 1929 hit. Most Mid Pines members considered it a "second club," and maintaining their primary membership elsewhere when bad times hit was challenge enough for many. People quit traveling as much to play golf, and Pine Needles' room counts dwindled. Both properties were hit—and hit hard.

Mid Pines drew only 3,413 room nights in 1929-30 (down more than twenty-five percent from 1928-29) and experienced its first operating loss—nearly $3,000. Room counts fell to fewer than 1,000 in 1932-33. Eldridge Johnson never softened to provide Richard Tufts additional capital for Pine Needles. The Tufts closed Pine Needles in 1931 and it sat idle for four years.

These were difficult times for Pinehurst Inc. It was challenge enough to maintain its resort compound and four golf courses in Pinehurst; but the drain in money and manpower for Mid Pines and Pine Needles exacerbated the problems. In fact, the experience of the Depression would forever linger menacingly in the minds of the Tufts. They moved very conservatively decades later, particularly when the physical plant needed overhauling in the 1960s. Instead borrowing money for much-needed work, they delayed it, insisting on doing only what cash flow allowed.

In his manuscript for an unpublished history of Pinehurst, Richard Tufts said the expansion toward Southern Pines, combined with bad economic times, "just about killed the goose that laid the golden egg. The dream (to develop Knollwood) brought Pinehurst to its knees in the early 1930s and would have brought an end to the ideals of its founder without the support of the Pinehurst cottage owners and the patience and wisdom of the Pinehurst creditor banks."

Things never got quite that bad. And as life around the Sandhills began to return to normal in the mid-1930s, Mid Pines and Pine Needles began the next chapters in their lives. Both impending eras were defined by successful businessmen who were regular visitors to the area for golf. Each saw opportunities to purchase distressed properties cheaply—and hopefully sell at nice profits later on.

John Sprunt Hill of Durham was a wealthy and influential businessman, banker (he founded Central Carolina Bank) and philanthropist in

One of the early lady golf greats was Glenna Collett, who honed her game at Pine Needles and sold real estate in its early years.

the early 1900s. One of his hobbies was golf, and he built the original Durham Country Club, later redesigned, expanded and renamed Hillandale Golf Club. He donated the course to the City of Durham in 1936. Hill was also an early member at Mid Pines.

Hill's son, George Watts Hill, roomed in a log cabin at the University of North Carolina in the late 1910s with David St. Pierre DuBose. Watts Hill and "Pete" DuBose became friends, and DuBose met and later married George's sister, Valinda. Years earlier, Hill had formed Homeland Investment Company to manage all of his real estate holdings, and he put his son-in-law atop the company as its president. Hill alerted DuBose, who was also an avid golfer, to a distressed property sale of Mid Pines in the fall of 1934. Ergo the involvement of Homeland Investment Company.

"I think it was a case of John Sprunt Hill being aware that the property was for sale, at probably a good price, discussing it with my father and things taking off from there," says David St. Pierre DuBose Jr., who still lives in Durham.

Homeland acquired the property for $90,000 at an auction on the Mid Pines Country Club front entry on November 8th, 1934. The club reopened the day after Christmas that year and was billed as a "clubhotel" in advertisements in the *Pinehurst Outlook*. Among the club's first guests were Hill and his wife and Watts Hill and his wife.

At the same time, another long-time winter resident of the Sandhills was taking an interest in resurrecting Pine Needles. George Dunlap Sr. was the prototypical Pinehurst guest, the one James Tufts had in his cross-hairs when he conceived the resort years before. Dunlap was a fabulously successful businessman in New York City—he and Alexander Grosset founded the famous publishing house of Grosset & Dunlap in 1898—but his health was never robust. The climate and recreational amenities in Pinehurst were Dunlap's prescription for about six months a year, beginning in 1908. He liked the experience so much he soon built a house on Beulah Hill Road named Broadview. He added a putting green in his backyard, and on that green his son, George Jr., began to develop the skills that would one day carry him to the 1933 United States Amateur championship and seven titles in the North and South Amateur.

Dunlap joined oil tycoon S.Y. Ramage of Oil City, Pennsylvania, and some silent investors to form Patuxent Development Company in early 1935 for the purpose of buying Pine Needles Inc., which had been declared bankrupt. The company bought Pine Needles and its

George Dunlap Jr. won six North & South Amateurs and helped his father run Pine Needles from the mid-1930s to the late 1940s.

five hundred and thirty-one acres on June 5th, 1935, for $75,000. Dunlap was named president and George Jr. was vice president.

"I am interested in the deal because I'm interested in anything that promises to help the section," Dunlap Sr. said. "A group of several Pinehurst winter residents, who have asked that their names not be published, have joined the enterprise."

The company spent $40,000 immediately on new roads, golf course reconditioning, a new children's playground and even a massive putting green like the one George Jr. had seen at Saint Andrews, Scotland. The eighteen-hole course included obstacles of tile pipes, croquet wickets and sprigs of pine trees.

The Hills and Dunlaps continued their enterprises through the rest of the decade, riding better times to reasonable levels of solvency. The greens at Pine Needles were converted from a sand/clay base to grass in 1937; Mid Pines' were converted the following year.

"Prosperity must be with us for we have a report that a twosome went out on the Mid Pines golf links the other day with three caddies, two to carry the bags and one to watch the ball go down the fairway—shades of boom days!" said a note in a 1937 *Sandhills Citizen.*

Just as the Depression changed the fibre of life in 1929, so too did America's entry into World War II in 1941. The Army Air Force immediately took over Mid Pines to house its Military Police personnel, and the Air Force Technical Training Command took over Pine Needles in April, 1942.

Business returned to normal following the war. Homeland Investment hired Frank and Maisie Cosgrove away from Pinehurst Country Club to run Mid Pines beginning in the fall of 1944. Patuxent continued to operate Pine Needles for three more years. But neither company ever realized the profits it had once envisioned.

"To run a resort and hotel requires a good bit of effort and talent," DuBose says of Mid Pines. "Homeland was not designed to run a resort. Its business was to invest in real estate and then dispose of the properties at a later date."

"Father just got tired of it. It was never a success," Dunlap Jr. says of Pine Needles. "I think they believed they could buy it cheap and later sell it at a profit. But it didn't turn out the way they expected."

Dunlap Jr., who lived in Naples, Florida, until his death in 2003, brokered a deal between Patuxent and the Roman Catholic Diocese of Raleigh, which needed a facility for a hospital and sanitarium. Pine Needles was purchased on June 4th, 1948, by The Reverend

Dunlap patterened this putting course behind the original Pine Needles Inn after the putting course he enjoyed at St. Andrews, Scotland.

Vincent S. Waters, Bishop of the Roman Catholic Diocese of Raleigh, for $406,000. The inn was renamed St. Joseph of the Pines and still is in operation today. Waters said the golf course would remain open for use by visitors and residents, and it did—for five years. Then the church tired of running a golf course and sold it in 1953 to the Cosgroves, their son-in-law and a golf-happy couple from Ohio.

In 1955, Homeland Investment wanted out of its ownership of Mid Pines. The company offered first dibs to the Cosgroves, who accepted and purchased the resort.

Mid Pines and Pine Needles were now in the hands of the families who would define their personalities today—the Cosgroves at Mid Pines and, across the street, a young couple named Warren and Peggy Kirk Bell. ∎

CHAPTER TWO

THE COSGROVES
OF MID PINES

F or fifty-one weeks a year, they go quietly about living their lives in towns like Allentown, Pennsylvania; Mansfield, Massachusetts; and Granby, Connecticut. They make fortunes and weather the hard times, celebrate marriages and births, send kids off to college, console those facing illness or divorce. They perform surgeries and try cases in the courtroom, they sell insurance policies and automobiles and shares of stock.

But for one week a year, they leave it all behind for a trip to Mid Pines Inn & Golf Club in Southern Pines, North Carolina.

The Souza group of twelve golfers has been coming the last week in March for forty-two years.

The Williams group of twenty has been coming the third week of March for thirty-six years.

And the Shuster group of from twelve to sixteen has been coming on the Friday after Thanksgiving for twenty-seven years.

They come because they like the playability of the golf course; two-handicappers enjoy it as do eighteen-handicappers. "Well, it's a Donald Ross," says Eric Shuster. "What else can you say?"

They like the familiar faces they've seen for many years—Charlie Riggin, the doorman; William Clarence, a distinguished bartender with a maroon jacket and bow tie; Dick Ferris, a long-time chef; caddies like Frank and Curtis; and some others who still work at Mid Pines like Allie Ray and Cynthia Elliott in the dining room.

They enjoy their thirty-six holes a day, their Nassaus and Stable-

TUFTS ARCHIVES

Frank "Pop" Cosgrove and wife Maisie always had a smile and a good word for their guests at Mid Pines from 1944-73.

fords, their greenies and sandies, the dollars that accumulate in the "Goof Pot" collected by one group for various transgressions—like topping a tee shot short of the ladies' tee or hitting a ball out-of-bounds. They love the total golf atmosphere. After all, if you want to know how priorities are really established at Mid Pines, the logo the club used for many years (featuring silhouettes of a golf bag, a golfer and a tennis player) was designed by a Boston girl visiting on her honeymoon. Her husband was playing golf at the time.

They love gathering in their rooms in the hotel or the living rooms of the Holly or Dogwood houses beside the tenth fairway along about six o'clock, just after their afternoon rounds, to commiserate over three-putts, skulled wedge shots and "what-ifs," to brag about that velvety six-iron shot and birdie putt—a cocktail in one hand, an hors d'oeurve in the other—and then repair to the dining room for a waist-expanding dinner. The groups who visit in March delight in getting pools and side bets together on the weekend's NCAA basketball tournament games.

It's a constant in their lives they won't do without.

"It's like a home away from home for a week," says John Souza, an automobile dealer in Massachusetts.

"It's a very special place," says Shuster, a stockbroker in Connecticut. "It has an ambiance that's unique. We've tried other places. But there was too much glitter or too much pretention. There's no place as comfortable as Mid Pines."

"It's a great escape from the phone, from your (medical) practice," says Dr. David Williams, a retired radiologist from Pennsylvania. "We just go down, relax and enjoy ourselves. My wife starts making roast beef and ham and corned beef for us to snack on a week before we go. I go loaded with a suitcase of food every year."

"It's spring. It's the end of winter," says Dr. Henry Fetterman, a member of the Williams party. "Sometimes when we leave Allentown, it might be snowing, raining, cold, windy. We get to Mid Pines in March and there's always something blooming. You can smell the springtime."

When Souza arrives each March, his first order of business, after checking in, is to make reservations for the following year. Is there ever any thought of trying another destination?

"Absolutley not," Souza says. "Never has anyone said we should go anywhere else. The day I arrive, I make reservations for next year. The day we leave, we start counting the days until we come back."

**

Like Pinehurst founder James Tufts before him, and like one-time

Babe Zaharias dressed for the holidays along with an unidentified Santa Claus during an early 1950s visit to Southern Pines.

Pine Needles owner George Dunlap before him as well, Frank Cosgrove was advised by his doctor as he neared middle-age to get out of the biting cold of New England in the winter. Cosgrove and his wife Maisie owned and operated the Gurnett Inn in Duxbury, Massachusetts, and "Pop," as everyone called him, was subject to getting pneumonia in cold weather.

A neighbor, Leon Murray, was manager of Pinehurst Country Club in the winter and needed some help, so he lured theCosgroves south for the beginning of the 1939 season. Pop worked as bartender and Maisie as a supervisor in the kitchen, and soon Pop became manager of the club's Out-of-Bounds Room—where members gathered for bridge, sandwiches and drinks. The Cosgroves and their three daughters, Louise, Jean and Ann, at first lived in a suite of rooms in the Pinehurst Country Club before moving into a house in the village.

A Corner of the Clubhouse

Pine Needles and Mid Pines were both shut down as resorts during World War II and used as bases for military personnel. But early in 1944, as the war was winding down, Homeland Investment Company of Durham, the owner of Mid Pines since 1934, was ready to reopen Mid Pines. Donald Ross, the eminent course architect at Pinehurst, knew that Homeland Investment would be needing a manager and suggested to the Cosgroves that Mid Pines might be a good opportunity for them. The Cosgroves liked the idea and worked out an arrangement to lease the facility from Homeland Investment. They signed the papers in May of 1944.

For the next twenty-nine years, the Mid Pines resort would be defined by the Cosgrove family.

And their first challenge was probably as tough a one as they'd encounter—that of simply getting the hotel and golf course open for the beginning of the 1944-45 season.

The Army Air Force took over Mid Pines to house Military Police personnel at the beginning of World War II, and the resort was in shambles when it left. Hay and wild grapes covered the golf course. Furniture was put in storage. The kitchen was in ruins. The interior of the hotel had been spray-painted Army beige, including all the brass fixtures and the ornate designs in the ceiling of the current lounge, "Cosgroves." To connect phone lines, the Army knocked holes in the walls and ran the wires through, exposed. Making matters worse was the fact that the soldiers apparently had a massive pillow fight during their last night in the hotel, as the Cosgroves found feathers all over the property the next day.

They faced a massive job in putting the hotel back in shape for paying customers. Furniture was returned from storage, the kitchen floor was replaced, and the kitchen equipment restored. The holes in the walls were replastered. There were draperies to clean, walls to paint, help to hire, supplies to order, uniforms to iron. The golf course needed work as well. The grass had grown to hip height. Grape plants were ripped out by attaching long chains with hooks on them and pulling them with tractors. The dam at the pond on the fifth hole was rebuilt, as golf ball scavengers had torn it up to allow all the water to drain out.

But the effort to open would be illustrative of the family affair Mid Pines would become.

"We put a lot of blood, sweat and tears into that place," said Jean Cosgrove Stevenson, who worked at Mid Pines during the season through her death in 2002. "It was a family operation. My sisters and I would spend twelve or fifteen hours a day working there. We worked the desk, waited tables, did maid work if we had to, or hostess work. We got to know all the guests and they got to know each other, and it almost became like a big family."

In 1953, the Cosgroves expanded their golf operations by becoming partners with their son-in-law, Julius Boros, and newlyweds Peggy and Warren Bell in purchasing the Pine Needles golf course across Midland Road. Warren operated the course on a day-to-day basis, as the Cosgroves had their hands full with Mid Pines and as Julius and Peggy played their respective pro golf tours. But when Homeland Investment was ready to sell Mid Pines two years later, it gave the Cosgroves the right of first refusal. Pop and Maisie needed their cash out of Pine Needles, so they sold their share to the Bells. On November 30th, 1955, they became full owners of Mid Pines.

Over the years, regular guests at Mid Pines have become enamoured of the many inviting features of the inn. None of its sixty-four rooms are alike. Many bathrooms, though recently renovated and modernized, still have original fixtures. To reach the guest rooms, you've got to traverse hallways that have settled into odd angles and that rise and fall in elevation in the wing over the dining room (that's so the dining room could have a high ceiling). There's also an old-fashioned game room that includes ping-pong tables, billiards, card tables and darts. The Cosgroves expanded the resort by building the "Golf-O-Tel," a ten-room lakeside villa, beside the fourth green in 1957, and by buying a half-dozen houses along Midland Road that border the tenth fairway. They also built meeting facilities to accommodate groups from out-of-town as well as local functions.

Captains of business, industry, politics and golf found the Cosgroves' service, Mid Pines' comfort and Donald Ross's ingenuity a luring combination. Among visitors over the years were Homer Cummings, attorney general of the United States; John O'Sullivan, Secretary of the Navy; Gene Zuckert, Secretary of the Army Air Force; Madame Von Trapp of *The Sound of Music* fame; and golf greats Sam Snead, Bobby Locke, Babe Zaharias, Arnold Palmer, George Bayer and Bob Toski, among others. Skip Alexander, the touring pro and American Ryder Cup team member in 1951, was head pro at Mid Pines from 1947-49.

Mid Pines drew many top ladies amateur players to its staff through the opportunity to play golf and practice during off-hours, including Mary Agnes Wall (Michigan state champion), Carol Diringer (Ohio state champion), Pat O'Sullivan (Connecticut state champion), Mae Murray (Vermont state champion), Kay Linnchan (New Hampshire state champion), Ruth Woodward Finch (Connecticut state champion), and Barbara McIntyre (North and South Amateur champion).

"My year at Mid Pines was one of the most wonderful of my life," says McIntyre, who worked there for the 1956-57 season. She had been friends on the ladies' amateur circuit with Peggy Bell and called her, looking for a job. The Bells didn't have anything at Pine Needles, so they sent her to the Cosgroves.

"I worked as a desk clerk and usually would have either the morning or the afternoon to play golf," she says. "I don't think you can beat a Donald Ross golf course."

These employees became, like many others, extensions of the Cosgroves' family.

"It wasn't like you were working there," says Ernie Boros, Julius's brother and his assistant pro at Mid Pines for twenty years from the early 1950s until the Cosgroves sold the resort in 1973. "And the guests, they

Golf exhibitions and tournaments drew enthusiastic crowds over the years to Mid Pines. Bobby Locke (top left) accepts winning check from Pop Cosgrove as Johhny Palmer and Skip Alexander look on; Jimmy Demaret tees off in photo at bottom.

45

got treated more like friends than paying customers."

"It's the only place I ever worked where the help had as much fun as the guests," says Jim Boros, Julius's nephew and a long-time golf shop staffer, assistant pro and later head pro. "During the season, you were working seven days a week. But no one ever complained."

Like the Bells at Pine Needles, with Peggy the public-relations and golf-instruction whiz and Bullet the operations man, the Cosgroves brought complementary skills and personalities to Mid Pines. The golf course was Pop's, the hotel was Maisie's. Though both consorted amicably with the guests, Pop was the one who played golf with the guests every day while Maisie was managing the staff and the books. Pop rarely raised his voice; when Maisie got her dander up, the employees steered clear.

"Pop was the kind of guy who never met a man he didn't like," says Jim Boros. "He'd take you under his wing, make you feel wanted. He did that with the entire staff."

"You'd never think he was the owner," says Nick Boros, Julius's oldest son. "He was right in there with the workers. He was friends with everybody."

Cosgrove grew up playing Marshfield Country Club, outside of Boston, so he had a keen appreciation for the game's history and tradition. He played left-handed, was known to hit a sweeping hook and usually shot between eighty and eighty-five.

"Dad had a love affair with the golf course," Jean says. "He'd spend the morning working on projects around the course, then play with the guests in the afternoon. He was a wonderful host. And he'd give the world away. One of the employees might come up and say, 'Gee, Mister Frank, it's been a bad day, could you loan me a few dollars?' Mother eventually had to say, 'No more, Frank, you're going to give away everything we've worked so hard for.'

"She was a strong person. When she spoke, that was it. She could do and did do anything around this hotel. In this business, you do what needs to be done, whether it's making up a bed or helping in the kitchen. That's what my mother was like. Nothing was beneath her. That rubbed off on the employees.

"Our life was Mid Pines," Jean continues. "At Christmas every year, Mom would say something like, 'Well, instead of a new mink coat this year, we'll get a walk-in refrigerator.'

"They were happy times, believe me."

Among employees who helped mold Mid Pines into the

Cosgroves' vision of the ideal resort was Dick Davenport, who spent twenty-seven seasons at Mid Pines from 1956-82, primarily as front-office manager.

"The Cosgroves were a fantastic success story," Davenport says. "They were in their fifties when they bought the resort, an age when most people are thinking about what they're going to do when they retire. The hotel was a mess, the golf course was a hayfield and they had no clientele when they first came over from Pinehurst."

The Cosgroves helped Davenport attend the prestigious hotel management program at Cornell University, but he says working under Maisie and Pop was all the learning he needed.

"I wouldn't trade all the classroom education in the world for what I learned from the Cosgroves in terms of how to treat the help and how to treat guests. They sure had the knack, and it was a pleasure to work for them," he says.

The prevailing spirit at Mid Pines has always been one of taking care of the guests first and having a little fun at the same time. Stories from Davenport and Pop Cosgrove illustrate those points.

Like other employees, Davenport worked long hours and confronted a variety of ticklish situations—like one that developed from the inn's lack of elevators. Davenport had booked the United Daughters of the Confederacy for a convention one year, and all the ladies were well along in years. The front desk staff wondered how to decide who got the second floor and who got the third.

"Start from the third," Davenport said. "That way we don't fill up the second, and if someone absolutely can't go to the third, we'll have room for her."

Soon a woman came to the desk and asked why she'd been put on the third floor.

Davenport thought quickly. "Ma'am, we're putting all the younger women on the third floor," he said.

The lady turned away, quite satisfied.

"I went back to the reservation office, about to break my arm patting myself on the back," Davenport says with a laugh. "Then I hear a roar from the lobby and the woman's back at the front desk."

"Where's that smooth-talking young man?" she demanded. "I think I've just been had."

Pop loved to work outside and one year decided all the bushes along the houses to the right of the tenth fairway needed trimming. He trimmed and chopped and raked for several days straight—and he was in his seventies at the time. One day a limousine pulled up and a well-to-do couple emerged. The man said they'd been watching him for a couple of days and were impressed with his skills and work ethic. "How's your situation here?" the man asked Cosgrove. "Are you happy? Would you consider a change?"

Pop didn't miss a beat. "Thanks, but no," he said. "I've been here a long time. They're nice people to work for."

He paused for effect, then added, "And besides, the old lady who owns the joint lets me sleep with her."

The Cosgroves were in their mid-seventies in the early 1970s. Neither Louise nor Jean was interested in buying the resort from their parents, and the threat of inheritance taxes to the daughters was daunting. So Pop and Maisie decided to look for a buyer.

Stuart Bainum, chief executive officer of Quality Inns International of Silver Spring, Maryland, was flying in his private plane from Atlanta back home one day around 1970 when he and his wife Jane decided to stop at the airport between Pinehurst and Southern Pines and explore the area. A fellow at the airport told him Mid Pines was a place he needed to visit.

"It was April and the dogwoods were blooming, and it's hard to beat Mid Pines that time of year," Bainum says.

The Bainums visited occasionally over the coming years and enjoyed the staff's attentiveness and the homey atmosphere. They heard it was for sale, and Bainum debated with himself over whether the property would be a good fit for Quality Inns.

"I told my wife I was not sure we could run it right," he says. "Even though it's hotel rooms and that's the business we're in, there was certainly a feel and personality to Mid Pines you don't get from a motel."

Despite his reservations, Bainum arranged for Quality Inns to buy the resort on February 28th, 1973, and the company ushered Mid Pines into the year-around resort business, installing air conditioning throughout the inn and public rooms. It also built four lighted tennis courts, a swimming pool and a new shuffleboard court and enlarged the pro shop.

Mid Pines remained one of the Sandhills' top golf resorts for another two decades. In 1987, Bainum stepped down as CEO as his son, Stuart Jr., took over. Several years later, the younger Bainum made the decision that if Quality Inns was going to keep Mid Pines, it needed to buy other resorts of its ilk and develop more expertise in the resort and golf business. The company made the decision not to go in that direction, however, and in the early 1990s, it started looking for a potential buyer for Mid Pines.

"In the end, it just wasn't a good fit," Bainum Sr. says. "Many people here were disappointed to see us sell it because it is a special place."

Across Midland Road at Pine Needles, a second golf course had been routed in 1989 by Pete and P.B. Dye and was to be part of a new club and residential community. But the Bell family held off actually building the course because of problems with environmental issues, the saturation of the Sandhills area with new golf development and the downturn of the United States economy in the early 1990s.

Durham native Skip Alexander was pro at Mid Pines from 1947-49 while playing on the pro tour.

Kelly Miller, general manager at Pine Needles and a son-in-law of Peggy Kirk Bell, made some inquiries of Quality Inn's parent company, Manor Care Incorporated, in 1993, about the possibility of purchasing Mid Pines. He learned that another interested party was long-time golf professional and course owner Sonny Ridenhour of Winston-Salem. The Bells joined Ridenhour and Jack Campbell of Winston-Salem and Jim Marsh of High Point in forming Mid Pines Development Group LLC and buying Mid Pines in March, 1994.

"I personally have thought that Mid Pines was as fine a golf course as Donald Ross ever built, and I've thought so for years," Ridenhour says.

"There was nothing like Mid Pines in the old days," says Mrs. Bell. "I've always thought it was so lovely. I've always loved playing there. It's a great golf course."

* * *

Though his day-to-day involvement with Mid Pines was cut short by the tragic and premature death of his wife, the former Ann "Buttons" Cosgrove, Julius Nicholas Boros was an important fixture in the Mid Pines landscape for many years.

Boros, who died in May, 1994, was a mainstay in professional golf for some three decades, earning entrance into the PGA World Golf Hall of Fame and winning two United States Opens and one

Ernie and Julius Boros (L-R, top) enjoy a good fish story; Julius later entered the World Golf Hall of Fame, while Buttons (above) was an accomplished amateur.

PGA Championship.

Curiously, though, Boros had not originally intended on being a golf pro. Boros was born in 1920 and was one of four sons and two daughters of Hungarian immigrants Lance and Elizabeth Boros. Julius (known to most close to him as Jay) was athletically gifted, having played high school golf and basketball and boxed while growing up in Fairfield, Connecticut, but he never showed the childhood genius at golf of, say, Jack Nicklaus. He didn't even take a concentrated interest in golf until he was twenty. His family was not wealthy, either; once Boros qualified for the United States Amateur, but he couldn't participate because travel expenses to California were prohibitive.

Boros received a degree in accounting from Bridgeport University and went to work for Roger Sherman Transfer Company in Hartford, which was owned and operated by a friend, Mike Sherman. Among the Sherman family's other holdings was Southern Pines Country Club, a twenty-seven-hole facility that originally was owned by the town of Southern Pines and first opened with a Donald Ross course in 1923. The club was a money-loser for the town, and it sold the course and buildings to Sherman in 1946; he owned it for five years until selling to the Southern Pines Elks Lodge in 1951. The Elks Lodge remains the owner today.

The winters were severe in Connecticut, and Boros complained that he had to put his clubs up for four months a year. Sherman needed some accounting help at Southern Pines, so he sent Julius south in the late 1940s, knowing that Boros could hone his golf game in his spare time and also give golf lessons to Sherman's wife, who spent much of the winter in Southern Pines.

Peggy Kirk, the amateur from Ohio, befriended Buttons Cosgrove on the winter golf circuit and often visited Southern Pines. She watched as a courtship developed between Jay and Buttons, who was quite an accomplished amateur golfer in her own right. (She was a former Massachusetts state champion and the winner of the 1949 Charlotte Open.)

"I don't remember exactly how Buttons and Jay met," Peggy says. "But we were all into golf and it wasn't exactly a big town. Jay was a very quiet man, very shy, he said very little. But Buttons was crazy about him. She'd say, 'Let's go over to Southern Pines Country Club and see Jay.' "

The more golf Boros played, the better he got. He once shot a 64 at Mid Pines in a pro-am, beating Ben Hogan and Sam Snead. He tied for second in the 1948 North and South Open and won the Shoreline Open that year. Boros wrestled with the issue of turning professional, with two ladies in his life on opposite sides of the issue.

"You'll starve, stick with your accounting," his mother told him. But Buttons wanted Jay to try the pro golf tour.

"She was the one who pushed him into turning pro," Peggy says. "Snead was at Mid Pines one time, and she said, 'Sam, you've got to talk Jay into turning pro. He's good, he can play, he ought to turn pro.' Skip Alexander was the pro at Mid Pines at the time. She got Skip to talk to Jay."

Boros soon took major steps professionally and personally. He relinquished his amateur status in December, 1949, and took over running the golf shop at Mid Pines while directing his competitive attentions to the PGA Tour. He and Buttons were then married, in May of 1950, and it was understandably a year of transition for Boros.

He won around $2,000 in prize money (a respectable sum at the time) and made a splash in the United States Open at Merion, shooting a 68 in the first round, leading it after forty-five holes and finishing ninth behind Hogan. It was the beginning of a distinguished record in the Open: Boros would win it twice and, from 1950-60, finish in the top five six times.

Boros improved to thirty-fourth in money winnings with $4,697 in 1951. He was tied for third at 219 with Paul Runyan after fifty-four holes of the 1951 Open at Oakland Hills, one shot behind Jimmy Demaret and Bobby Locke. Hogan was a shot back and eventually won, but Boros was bouyed by his fourth-place finish.

Soon after, tragedy struck. Buttons died at the age of twenty-three in the hospital in Boston, Massachusetts, on September 9th, 1951, just a day after giving birth to Nick (the Boroses had been at their summer home on the south shore of Massachusetts, waiting for the baby to arrive). Jay was devastated but had to go on with his life. He immersed himself in his golf game and, while the Cosgroves looked after the baby, he took off at the beginning of the 1952 season to conquer the pro golf tour.

Hogan was the defending U.S. Open champion when it came to Northwood Country Club in Dallas in June, 1952. He opened with rounds of matching sixty-nines, and Boros was four shots behind with a pair of seventy-ones as the thirty-six hole Open Saturday began. Boros shot a sixty-eight in the morning and vaulted ahead of Hogan's seventy-four. A seventy-one in the afternoon gave Boros a 281 total and an easy margin over Porky Oliver at 285 and Hogan at 286.

The year was a good one for golfers with North Carolina ties, as Boros won the U.S. Open, Harvie Ward of Tarboro won the British Amateur, Johnny Palmer of Badin won the Canadian Open, and Dick Chapman of Pinehurst won the French Amateur. A homecoming tournament and celebration was held at Mid Pines in November, with Richard Tufts, vice president of the United States Golf Association, presenting an award from the state of North Carolina honoring the quartet. Snead shot rounds of 68-67-70 to win the fifty-four hole tournament.

Boros was three months past his forty-third birthday when the 1963 Open traveled to The Country Club in Brookline, Massachusetts. Boros finished seventy-two holes at 293 and was cleaning his locker out, expecting Jacky Cupit to hang on to a two-shot win through his seventieth hole. But Cupit made a six on the seventeenth hole, forcing a tie with Boros and Arnold Palmer at 293. Boros won the playoff the next day with a seventy to Cupit's seventy-three and Palmer's seventy-six. He was the second oldest ever to win the tournament (behind Ted Ray, who was a few months older in 1920).

Boros was a four-time member of the Ryder Cup and capped his career by winning the 1968 PGA Championship at Pecan Valley Country Club in San Antonio, Texas. He got up and down from off the green on the seventy-second hole to beat Palmer and Bob Charles by one stroke. He was inducted into the World Golf Hall of Fame in 1982, having won eighteen professional tournaments.

Those who knew his game say if Boros could have made a few more putts, there's no telling how much he might have won.

"He was never known as a super putter from ten to twelve feet in," says Jim Boros. "He was best on hard golf courses, where shot-making was demanded and it wasn't just a putting contest for a lot of birdies."

"I don't usually putt too well," Julius admitted. "In fact, I'm mediocre at it."

Boros had an memorable personality and style on the golf course. Brother Ernie remembers him as being "quiet, very quiet" as a kid, and that pretty much defined his adulthood as well. Boros was described on various occasions as being relaxed, serene, poker-faced, plodding. He was a large man, and his lumbering style prompted nicknames such as "The Moose" and "The Bear." Others called him "Big Jules" or "Big Julie." *Sports Illustrated* featured him once and titled the story "Old Man

River," another name that stuck. His mouth was generally working on a cigarette or a blade of grass.

He wasted no time on the golf course. Growing up on a farm alongside a golf course, Boros would often jump the fence and play a few holes before getting run off, mindful of the point that fast golf meant more golf. He planned his shot walking up to the ball—which club to hit, what kind of ball flight, where to land the shot. It was a kind of "golf polo," as *Sports Illustrated* once termed it.

Boros felt a practice swing a waste of time and energy and instead gripped the club in his right hand and practiced a quick "release"—the motion he'd soon make at impact. He always kept something in motion as he set up to the ball—a foot, a shoulder, an arm—so as not to tighten up. As soon as he hit the golf ball, he'd start walking toward it, thinking about the next shot.

Boros's easy-going demeanor reflected his outlook. "How many times have you played with someone who has missed a shot, lost his temper and, because of it, missed the next shot, too?" Boros once said. "There is nothing sillier than this. You know when you leave the clubhouse and head for the first tee that you are going to hit a certain number of bad shots, so learn to accept them."

Boros characterized himself as a "swinger," not a "hitter" like Nicklaus and Palmer. "If I tried to muscle the ball like Palmer and Nicklaus do, I'd be home in Fort Lauderdale for most of the year."

"Rhythm, that Boros's secret," Claude Harmon once said. Tony Lema said it was "all hands and wrists, like a man dusting the furniture."

The true love of his life beyond his family was fishing. Boros once responded to a question about his plans to retire with, "Retire from what? All I do is play golf and fish." He checked every pond and lake on a golf course as a potential fishing site for later in the day, and the lake beside the fourth hole at Mid Pines was a favorite spot. Julius once fell in that lake while fishing and tried to sneak into the clubhouse without being spotted.

During GGO weeks, Boros always stayed at Mid Pines and com-
muted to Greensboro. He'd spend hours hitting bunker shots out beside
the eighteenth green and hitting hundreds of balls down the first fairway
from a practice tee in front of the real tee.

For a while, Julius maintained an apartment at the Cloverleaf Apart-
ments (now the Palmetto House) in Pinehurst. In 1955, he married an
airline stewardess named Armen Boyle and they took Nick and moved
to Fort Lauderdale, where they had six more children. Nick is a golf
teaching pro in Hollywood, Florida. Another of the Boros's sons, Guy,
is on the PGA Tour today.

Nick remembers spending time during the summers with his grandparents, with Aunt Louise and Aunt Jean and their husbands and his cousins.
The three families lived in three houses in a row along the tenth fairway
and green (today the Azalea, Camelia and Dogwood cottages). He grew
up with golf and went to the University of Iowa on a golf scholarship.

"I studied hotel management because I thought one day I'd come back
and be involved with the hotel," he says. "Unfortunately, my grandparents sold it so I never got the chance."

Nick brought his son and daughter back to Mid Pines in 1993 to play
in a golf tournament, and old-timers around the resort were amazed at
his resemblance to Pop Cosgrove.

"I saw the photo of him on the wall and couldn't believe the similari-
ties," he says. "I've got the same glasses, the same receding hairline. I
definitely favor the Cosgrove side of the family."

He was heartened when Peggy Bell told him the new owners' goal
was to run Mid Pines today like his grandparents did decades ago.

* * *

Each year at the Williams party's final dinner gathering, David
Williams gives everyone a chance to voice an opinion on the
following year's destination.

"All right, gentlemen, what will it be next year?" he might ask.
"Should we try Myrtle Beach? Hilton Head? Do we want to go somewhere in Florida?"

Inevitably, someone will answer: "I say we come back here."

"All right, let's put it to a vote," Williams says.

And the tally is always, as it has been for more than three decades,
twelve to nothing—in Mid Pines' favor.

"We've sold this idea to a fair number of people in Allentown. I can
think of three or four groups that started taking trips much the same

A welcome sight: the entrance to Mid Pines Inn off Midland Road.

as ours," Williams says. "They've gone to Doral, Myrtle Beach, different places. The funny thing is, though, none of those groups have stayed together."

John Souza and three golf buddies picked Mid Pines straight out of an advertisement in *Golf Digest* back in the early-1950s. In the early days, they rode the train to Southern Pines, where a driver from the inn would pick them up. They've lived through the evolution of the golf cart and the subsequent demise of the caddie, through the Cosgrove era, the Quality Inns era and now the new era of the Mid Pines-Pine Needles ownership union.

"We've seen a little of everything," Souza says. "It's like old-home week when we go back down there."

Eric Shuster agrees.

"I was introduced to Mid Pines by a friend who'd been coming since the 1940s," says Shuster. "He's now ninety-six years old. The last time he went to Mid Pines was three years ago, and he played eighteen holes a day at age ninety-three. Now my nephew has joined our group. He's thirty-one. I hope he'll keep the tradition up long after I'm not going anymore. I think he will. He loves it there as much as the rest of us."

Each group has a waiting list, but openings rarely develop. Souza runs a tight ship, in fact, and unsavory behavior by a newcomer— drinking too much or an overbearing attitude toward the staff are among the sins can get a golfer black-balled for the next year.

One week before the Souza group leaves for Southern Pines each March, the golfers gather at the Brook Manor Pub in Attleboro, Massachusetts, for a pre-trip dinner. Souza hands out plane tickets and announces room assignments and pairings for the various competitions they'll play. Over steaks, chops and lobsters and a few bottles of good wine, the group eagerly anticipates its pending adventure.

"They've been having this dinner for twenty-five years," says the restaurant owner, Bob Scarlatelli. "They have a wonderful time. We feel like we're related. We look forward to having them as much as they enjoy coming here."

Scarlatelli said that, yes, he's a golfer himself and that, yes, he'd like to join the group some day if they had an opening and an invitation. "But being in the restaurant business, I'd never have the time," he said, a twinge of regret in his voice. ■

CHAPTER THREE

THE BELLS
OF PINE NEEDLES

Peggy Kirk Bell and her husband Warren stood on the corner outside Joe Montesanti's drugstore on Broad Street in Southern Pines that summer afternoon in 1957. Little by little, their dreams were falling apart. Life was throwing them curve balls, shanks and fat wedge shots.

The Bells owned a golf course about a mile away named Pine Needles, but their lease was about to run out on the buildings which they used to house and feed the men who played their course. The owner of the buildings wasn't interested in extending the lease, and the Bells had little money of their own, having cashed in some life insurance and borrowed money from Peggy's father to buy the golf course from their original partners two years earlier. They desperately needed $100,000 to build twenty rooms.

Bullet had already tried unsuccessfully to get a loan from a bank to build some lodges and a clubhouse. The tension was getting thick. Their lease was up in a year, and what good was a resort golf course if you couldn't provide visitors a place to sleep and eat? Peggy thought that she could talk the bank into loaning them the money they needed, but she'd failed as well.

"It's insane," she cried. "It makes no sense at all. We've got a good, loyal clientele. There are no liens on the golf course. Why are we having so much trouble getting the money?"

"I don't know," Bullet said. "So what do we do now?"

Peggy and Warren Bell created Pine Needles in their own image.

About this time a friend in the insurance business named Jimmy Hobbs passed by. He saw the forlorn expressions on the Bells' faces. The Bells told him about their problem. Hobbs nodded his head. "I'll see if I can get you the money," he said and walked off.

"What was that all about?" Peggy asked.

"He's just trying to cheer us up," Bullet said.

One week later, Hobbs called the Bells. "A man named Frank Houston of Occidental Life Insurance in Raleigh is coming down to meet you and play golf," he said. "He might be able to help with your problem."

Houston drove down to Southern Pines and was given a tour of Pine Needles by the Bells. He saw the grand hotel at the top of the hill built by the Tufts family of Pinehurst Incorporated in the late 1920s, the one that fell into the abyss of the Great Depression. The original Pine Needles Inn was bought by the Catholic Diocese of Raleigh in the late-1940s and was now a hospital named St. Joseph of the Pines. Houston saw the old Army barracks named "The Golfery" on one side of the hotel with community baths and cots that housed the golfers from Albany and Syracuse, the Bronx and Queens, Dayton and Toledo after their thirty-six-hole-a-day marathons on the Pine Needles golf course. He saw the clubhouse building which included the golf shop, locker rooms and dining room.

In the course of the day, Houston learned of the love for golf shared by Peggy and Bullet, how their first date had been on the golf course (Peg dusted him and won a trip to the movies); how Bullet retired from pro basketball and went into selling golf clubs for Spalding; how Bullet was nicknamed because he darted so swiftly through quarries and swimming pools as a youngster; of Peggy's days on the fledging LPGA Tour, her friendship with Babe Zaharias, her win in the 1949 Titleholders (the day's women's equivalent of the Masters). He saw the fire in their bellies that stoked their eighteen-hour work days.

Bullet told Houston how, to save money, he'd supervise the construction himself. "I've already drawn the plans," said Bell, adding that he had studied mechanical drawing in high school. "I'll buy the materials, hire the carpenters."

The Bells showed him the strip of land between Midland Road and the second hole of the golf course, an uphill par-five, where they dreamed of building a series of lodges and a clubhouse. They'd recently purchased twenty acres for $20,000 and felt the site ideal to relocate Pine Needles' resort operation.

Bullet pointed to the first hole of the golf course, a difficult, downhill par-four.

"This would become the eighteenth if we built a clubhouse down there," he said. "It would be a great finishing hole. Then we make the second hole the first hole. The third hole becomes the second, and so on. Otherwise, we don't change anything about the golf course."

Houston was impressed. At day's end, he had an announcement to make. "I'll loan you the money," he said.

Bullet was hoping to get the commitment in writing. "We've had a bunch of promises that fell through," he said.

"I'll call you tomorrow," Houston said.

And he did.

Thus began the modern era of Pine Needles Lodge & Golf Club.

With that $100,000, the Bells built the four lodges that stand to the right of the clubhouse as you look at them from the first tee of the golf course—$20,000 for each five-room lodge and $20,000 more for furniture.

"That got us going. That was a tremendous relief," Peggy says. "I'm not sure we knew what we were getting into. All we'd ever wanted to do was own a golf course. Now we were in the hotel business for good."

* * *

Peggy Kirk's eighteenth summer didn't seem to hold much promise. She'd hoped to go to summer camp in New Hampshire, as she did every year, and swim and canoe and hike, but her mother said she was too old for camp. Findlay, Ohio, was a nice enough little town, some twenty thousand people working and raising families in the shadow of a huge Marathon Oil headquarters about an hour south of Toledo and Lake Erie. But it was hardly chock full of excitement for a recent high-school graduate.

"What am I supposed to do all summer?" she cried in frustration one night at the dinner table.

Robert Kirk had an idea. A friend of his had recently moved to Texas and needed to sell his membership at Findlay Country Club. Kirk, who owned a series of three grocery warehouses in northwest Ohio and a sporting goods store in Findlay, thought the club might be fun for his family—wife Grace, twins David and Grace, age twenty, and Peggy, eighteen—and bought the fellow's membership.

"You can learn to play golf if you'd like," he told Peggy.

JOHN HEMMER

Bullet and Peggy Bell, newlyweds and new co-owners of Pine Needles, arrive in Southern Pines on Peggy's plane in 1953.

"Golf?" Peggy said. She was vaguely familiar with the game, having swung a few clubs baseball-bat style at summer camp, but she didn't know a birdie from a bogey. Yet it was still something to do.

She picked up a set of clubs and got three balls from her father's sporting goods store and went to the club for a round of golf. Technique? Rules? Who cares, she thought. Peggy just wanted to play.

She never made it to the first green.

Peggy lost all three balls in the woods. Dejected and confused, she trudged back to the clubhouse, where she found the golf professional, Leonard Schmutte. Peggy gripped a golf club like a baseball bat and asked if that was the correct way to hold the club.

"Not exactly," Schmutte said. "Would you like a golf lesson?"

"Yes," Peggy answered. "Can we go right now?

"I'm afraid not," he said. "I have to mind the shop. But you be here at nine o'clock in the morning."

Over the summer of 1939, Peggy Kirk fell in love with the game of golf. Schmutte taught her grip, stance, alignment, swing

Peggy Kirk takes a lesson from Leonard Schmutte, the Findlay Country Club pro who introduced her to the game.

plane, follow through, footwork, chipping, pitching, putting, sand play, course management. She hit balls all day, every day, then played late in the afternoon. Lessons cost fifty cents, but Schmutte never charged her a dime.

"I couldn't get enough," she says. The game eventually came fairly easily to Peggy, who always excelled at athletic pursuits, although there was the tendency in the beginning to force her strength and athletic ability on the golf ball.

"I'd miss the ball and Leonard would say, 'Good swing.' I'd think, 'I don't care how my swing looks, I want to hit it long and straight.' I was forcing it, trying to muscle it out there. I hit those balls literally every direction imaginable," Peggy says.

Her goal at the time was to attend Sargeant's Physical Education School in Boston (now a part of Boston University) to study for a career in teaching. That went well enough for two years, until she visited her parents in Florida while the northeast was choked in a blizzard. "I got sunburned in Florida while it was snowing in Boston," she said. "I thought, 'Why don't I transfer to a Florida school, where I can play golf all year?'"

Peggy made the move to Rollins College in Winter Park before the 1941 school year began. In the warm climate of the Sunshine State, her golf game flourished. She played every tournament she could find, and one day she saw a notice in the newspaper about the North and South Women's Amateur in a place called Pinehurst.

"Pinehurst," she said. "That's supposed to be the golf capital of the world. Gosh, I need to go play in that tournament."

So she bundled up some clothes, tossed her golf clubs into her Packard convertible and set off for Pinehurst. She arrived without mishap, found the country club and presented herself at the tournament desk in the clubhouse.

"I'd like to enter the North and South," she said. "What is the entry fee?"

The tournament official said: "There is no entry fee. This is an invitational tournament."

"Invitational?" Peggy responded, her freckles turning bright red. "I'm sorry, gee, I'm just a college kid, I read about it and thought I'd like to play in it."

"Just a moment," said the official, who excused himself into a rear office. A moment later, while Peggy was looking for a convenient rug under which to crawl, a distinguished looking man with wire-rimmed glasses presented himself.

"Hello," he said. "I'm Richard Tufts, and I'd like to extend an invitation to you to play in the North and South."

"My first trip to Pinehurst, and I crash the party," Peggy says today. "I was so green."

Among the friends Peggy made playing in her first North and South was a young woman named Ann Cosgrove, nicknamed "Buttons" because her eyes at birth were tiny, perfect circles that resembled buttons. At the time, Ann's parents were employees of the Carolina Hotel (today the main hotel at Pinehurst Resort & Country Club), but soon would move to Southern Pines to take over management of Mid Pines Country Club. Peggy and Ann's friendship flourished, and over the next few years, as Peggy graduated from college and began playing the women's amateur circuit regularly, she'd visit Mid Pines every year between Thanksgiving and Christmas to work on her golf game. "There was nothing like Mid Pines in the old days," Peggy says. "I've always loved playing there. The hotel and golf course were so lovely."

Times were different then. There was an esprit d'corps among the girls that was unique. Carol Johnson, a long-time friend of Mrs. Bell's who's a regular teacher at the Pine Needles Golfaris, first met Peggy when Peggy squirted water in her face at Columbus Country Club in 1946. The girls short-sheeted Peggy's bed and tied her pajamas in knots one year at the Ohio State Women's Amateur. Peggy won the tournament and the joke for years after that was, "You better find out where I'm staying so you can short-sheet my bed."

Peg's all smiles in 1949 after beating Clair Doran for her third straight Ohio Open.

Once Carol and mates bought a live lobster and put it in Peggy's bathtub on the sixteenth floor of a hotel in Chicago during the Western Amateur. "Look what came up through the pipe!" Peggy squealed. The others rolled on the floor, near tears.

They're still playing jokes. Not long ago, Peggy woke up on her seventy-third birthday to find seventy-three pumpkins delivered to her front yard along the eighteenth fairway at Pine Needles.

"We were a close-knit group," says Ann Casey Johnstone, another long-time instructor at Golfaris. "We weren't in it for the glory. All we got was our names in the papers. There was no money to be won turning pro. Our fields in amateur tournaments were much deeper than now. Today, all the good players turn pro."

Meanwhile, Warren Bell was a three-time All-State basketball player and a local celebrity in Findlay. Peggy was at home from Florida after playing the women's amateur golf tour in May, 1944, and driving down the street in her convertible when she saw Bullet standing on the street corner. They'd known each other since childhood—"He was my boyfriend in third grade," Peggy says—and he'd heard of Peggy's love of golf.

"Hey, Kirkie," Bell said. "I hear you've been playing in some golf tournaments. You must be pretty good now. Bet I could beat you."

"Like to try?" Peggy responded.

"We'll bet a movie," said the cocky Bell, who knew little about golf. "I win, you take me. You win, I take you."

Peggy won handily, and a leisurely courtship ensued that would last nearly a decade and span Warren's three-year stint with the Fort Wayne Pistons of the NBA and Peggy's continued climb in amateur and then pro golf circles. By 1953, Peggy had turned pro and Warren was a Spalding equipment salesman. He was ready to get married. Peggy loved him but wasn't sure about the commitment. Bullet eventually convinced Peggy into setting a date, which they did, August 15th, 1953.

"He wanted to get married or get on with his life," Peggy says. "I was very, very shy at the time. That's why golf has been good for me. You gain confidence in all areas of your life if you do well in one."

They planned a small service with only a few members of the immediate family present. Everyone showed up except Peggy, who took her cold feet to the air in her Cessna for a ride over the countryside. "You could lose yourself up there," she says. "The freedom you felt was unlike anything else."

She returned to earth, searched her soul for three days and finally called Bullet.

"Bullet, do you still want to get married?" she asked.

"Who is this?" he barked into the phone.

They were married that afternoon and joked for years and years that they had a pseudo-anniversary, August 15th, and a real one, August 18th.

* * *

How appropriate is it that Peggy Kirk Bell would one day own the golf course on which the first women's open tournament was ever held? That Peggy's career would be profoundly influenced by one of the organizers and the eventual runner-up of that tournament? That thousands of ladies have improved their games over the years at Mrs. Bell's trademarked Golfaris? And that the 1996, 2001 and 2007 United States Women's Opens were held at Pine Needles?

You be the judge.

Of course, at the time of Pine Needles' first tournament in 1928, Peggy Kirk was a seven-year-old growing up in Ohio and had no idea

U.S. Professional Weathervane team members (L-R) Betty Bush, Betsy Rawls, Peggy Kirk, Betty Jamison, Patty Berg and Babe Zaharias board plane for 1951 trip to Great Britain.

who Glenna Collett was. But Miss Collett was a key figure in an important development unfolding in the Sandhills of North Carolina.

Readers of the sports pages of *The New York Times* might have noticed the following headline on the section front the morning of Sunday, January 8th, 1928:

Women's First Open Golf Play in History
Set for Pinehurst; Miss Browne is Listed.

The story mentioned that eighteen holes of qualifying followed by match play would begin on February 1st at Pine Needles. Miss Collett was a member of the organizing committee. Mary K. Browne was a top professional expected to enter, and Maureen Orcutt and Virginia Van Wie were among quality amateurs expected to compete. "The time is ripe for such an event," the organizers proclaimed, noting that a number of top lady golfers were now professional (though it would be some twenty years before an organized circuit of tournaments would develop) and a competition needed to be held among all women golfers. Miss Collett won the qualifying medal, shooting eighty, and finished second to Miss Van Wie in the tournament.

Fast forward to 1950.

Peggy Kirk has learned to play golf. And learned quite well. Already in her eleven-year-old golf career, she's won three Ohio Opens (from 1947-49), the 1949 North and South Amateur, the 1949

68

Titleholders, teamed to win the the Hollywood Four-Ball with Babe Zaharias and been named an alternate on the 1948 Curtis Cup team. And now she's achieved her paramount goal: full membership on a United States Curtis Cup team. The captain of the 1950 team which would play Great Britain and Ireland at the Country Club of Buffalo was Glenna Collett Vare. She was enjoying the twilight of an outstanding career that included six wins in the U.S. Women's Amateur from 1922-35. Though she was past her competitive prime when young Peggy Kirk came along, the latter worshipped the former for her ability and what she'd meant to women's golf. Glenna was also renowned for a certain other ability—that of finding four-leaf clovers.

"Everyone knew she had this special gift," Peggy says. "Maybe that's why she was such a great putter—she could see the lines and slopes so clearly."

The United States team had a 2-1 lead after the first day's foursomes competition. Peggy was somewhat distraught at having lost, along with Helen Sigel, to their opponents from the British Isles. That night, Peggy was petrified at the thought of playing singles the next day.

"I was nervous about playing for my country," she says. "I said, 'Please don't play me.'"

"Glenna told me, 'I call the shots. I'm the captain. And you're playing.'"

Peggy was on the sixteenth fairway the next day in her match against Jeanne Bisgood when her captain approached.

"How do you stand?" Glenna asked.

"I'm one-down," Peggy said.

Glenna walked off and then returned to Peggy in a couple of minutes. She handed Peggy a four-leaf clover and said, "Go get her."

Peggy did, winning seventeen and eighteen for a 1-up triumph as the U.S. team prevailed, 7½ to 1½.

That gesture probably sums up Peggy Kirk Bell's life in golf as much as any. The woman has had a four-leaf clover since the day she learned to play golf.

Peggy graduated from Rollins in 1943 and returned to assist in the war effort at home in Findlay. At the end of World War II, she was free to travel the loosely organized tour of women's events that included five amateur tournaments in Florida, the national Amateur, the Western Amateur and Open, the Women's Texas Open, the All-American and World Open at Tam O'Shanter, the North and South, the Tampa

The flying golfer takes off for another excursion to the LPGA Tour.

Open and the Titleholders Championship.

She turned pro after the Curtis Cup in September 1950, and was given $10,000 a year by Spalding. She played the 1951 tour as it started in Florida and crossed the country to New Orleans, Texas, Phoenix, Las Vegas and into California. Peggy enjoyed the life—except for the long drives.

The world of airplanes and flying fascinated Peggy since childhood and she even wanted to go to flight school during World War II—"Learn to fly at the government's expense," she says. But her application was rejected because she was red-green color blind. Still, the lure of the air was omnipresent and, in early 1952, she had the opportunity to quench that thirst for flight.

Peggy commiserated in New Orleans with Gloria Armstrong, an amateur friend from California, about her dread of driving across the country to California again that year.

"If I were a pro, I'd sure fly from tournament to tournament," said Gloria, who could fly and even owned her own plane. "Say, Peggy, why don't I teach you to fly?"

"Now that would be fun," Peggy said.

Gloria taught Peggy to fly as they headed westward and helped her buy her airplane, a Cessna that cost $8,000 at a dealership in Dallas. She flew the golf tour coast to coast in following years and, after Bonnie's birth in 1954, sometimes took Bonnie and her nurse with her. Babe Zaharias was a frequent travel partner as well. Peggy made a lot of friends among fellow pilots, and she and Bullet held the first Pilots National Golf Championship at Pine Needles in 1955. Entrants had to have a valid pilot's license to play in the thirty-six hole tournament, which was won by the vaunted amateur golfer, Frank Stranahan of Toledo, Ohio.

Peggy had several harrowing experiences, the last of which grounded her for good. Peggy was flying from Findlay to Southern Pines in 1959 when a snowstorm moved in. She had to fly low and use a railroad for navigation as she flew over Virginia.

A devout Christian, Peggy said a little prayer that frigid afternoon, hoping to make it home to her husband and two little girls. "God, if you get me down safely I promise I'll never fly a plane again," Peggy whispered.

Eventually, she saw an open field, did a 180-degree turn and landed the plane. She kept her word. Peggy sold the plane and used the proceeds to build the swimming pool at Pine Needles.

Much of her career would be marked by her close friendship to Mildred Didrickson Zaharais, better known by her nickname of "Babe"— acquired after she hit five home runs once in a baseball game. Their friendship began when they met at the 1945 Western Women's Open. Babe's mother had just died, and Peggy expected her to withdraw. But she didn't. "I'm going to win this for my mother," she said—and of course did.

Two years later, Babe asked Peggy to be her partner in the Hollywood Four-Ball. "I need a partner, and you may as well win a tournament," Babe told her. Later, when Peggy was shaking with nerves before the tournament, Babe told her: "I can beat any two of them without you. I'll let you know if I need you."

They won the tournament, one of seventeen in a row Babe won in 1946 and 1947. In her career, Babe would win ten major championships and thirty-one tournaments total.

Peggy has so many memories of Babe: of playing with Sam Snead one day from the same tees, Babe outdriving Snead on one hole and Snead accusing her of playing a souped-up ball; their frequent rounds

PINE NEEDLES LODGE & GOLF CLUB

Babe Zaharias signed Peggy's charter membership card to the LPGA in April, 1951.

and lessons with Tommy Armour during wintertime in Boca Raton; of the Babe's svelte touch on the greens, her ability to make five-footer after five-footer; of her abilities and interests beyond the golf course—to play the harmonica, to cook, to type, to dance, to do almost anything and do it well.

"We'd be on the road and she'd be ironing a blouse, and she'd say, 'I'm the best ironer there is.' And she probably was. That was the Babe," Peggy says. "She was so confident. She didn't seem conceited. It was just a case of somebody being talented enough to do what they said they were going to do.

"In golf, she was so much better than anyone else. She could hit it so far. She used to say, 'I wish these girls would get better. Then I'd have to go practice.' "

Her cockiness could alienate other golfers on the fledging LPGA Tour. Several golfers took exception to the Babe's boasting, gamesmanship and sometimes overbearing personality and once complained about extra appearance money Babe got from various tournaments. Babe got wind of the rumbling and, as president of the LPGA, called a membership meeting.

"I'm the star of this show and all of you are in the chorus," she said. "I get the money and if it weren't for me, half of our tournaments wouldn't even be."

"I told her, 'Babe, you shouldn't have said that. I would have said it for you.' " Peggy says. "But she was right. And that was the Babe. She was totally honest and said what she thought."

Peggy remembers sitting in hotel rooms in the late-1940s and listening as Babe negotiated over the phone with tournament organizers—turning what could have been simply clinics for her into tournaments for her and the others.

You never know whose famous face you might see at Pine Needles. Above, Michael Jordan pauses with Peggy Bell and Pat McGowan after a round. Below, Michael Campbell relaxes with the Bell family after winning the 2005 U.S. Open at Pinehurst; Campbell stayed at Pine Needles that memorable week in June 2005.

"They'd offer her $500 or $1,000 for the appearance, so she'd say, 'I'll tell you what. You put up $2,000, and I'll come and bring a bunch of girls with me. I'll keep $500 and the girls will play for $1,500," Peggy says. "And all of a sudden, you've got a tournament.

"She was the founding force behind the LPGA Tour. Without her, it wouldn't have happened. When Babe died, the tour dwindled for a while. Thanks to Patty Berg and Louise Suggs, the tour kept going, then it took off again when Mickey Wright came along."

Babe was a frequent visitor to Pine Needles and enjoyed competing with Bullet at billiards, ping-pong, golf and anything else with a winner at the end. "Both were fierce competitors," Peggy says.

She was Bonnie Bell's godmother and told Peggy just after the birth that she assumed Peggy would name the baby after her.

"Name the baby 'Mildred?'" Peggy cried. "You don't even like 'Mildred.'"

"No, I mean 'Babe.' It'll sound great in the papers: 'Babe Bell.'"

Peggy remembers her last round with Babe as the final stages of back cancer gripped her in the mid-1950s. They played at Tampa Country Club, and Babe, her swing weakened by illness and medication, could only knock her tee shots as far out as Peggy.

"After five holes, Babe said to me, 'Peggy, you sure are a great golfer. How can you break eighty hitting it so short?'" Peggy remembers. "She was used to hitting an eight-iron when I was hitting a five-iron."

Babe died in 1956, and by the late-1950s Peggy was about ready to withdraw from regular competition on tour to devote more time to her family and resort in Southern Pines. A number of years later, the LPGA Tour made its first-ever visit to the Pinehurst area for the 1972 Titleholders, which was played at Pine Needles. Then in 1995, the Pinewild Women's Championship was played at Pinewild. Playing both days in the pro-am was Peggy Bell, seventy-four years old, going on twenty-one.

"Peggy didn't care what the world thought of her," says Hollis Stacy, a veteran LPGA Tour pro. "She went out and helped start this tour. She's a non-conformist. It helps to have people like that, to help lay the groundwork for the LPGA. I admire her for having the fortitude. Playing golf wasn't the typical fashion for women back then. I'm very thankful we had pioneers of that sort."

* * *

Peggy Kirk and Bullet Bell knew they wanted to be in the golf

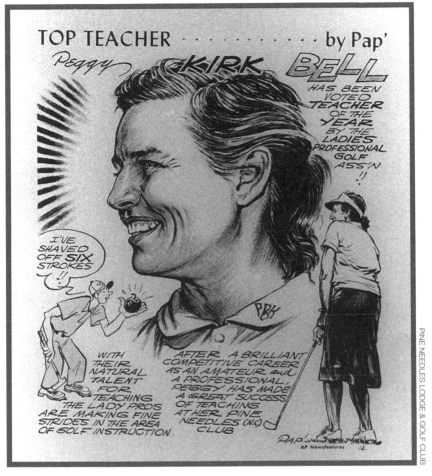

business. They wanted to own and operate a golf course. So as their wedding in the summer of 1953 neared, they spent considerable time exploring their options. They thought of building a course in Findlay. They also thought of buying or building in Florida. While Peggy was playing tournament golf in Florida that winter, Bullet scouted several courses in the area they might buy.

It so happened that winter that at one tournament Peggy ran into her old friends from North Carolina, Maisie and Frank Cosgrove. The Cosgroves had been running Mid Pines Country Club in Southern Pines for nine years, and Peggy had spent many wonderful times there.

The reunion was bittersweet, however. They all still ached over the tragic death in September, 1951, of Buttons Cosgrove, the youngest of the three Cosgrove girls. Buttons had married an unknown golf pro named Julius Boros in 1950 and had given birth to a son, Nick, early in the fall of 1951. She died of a cerebral hemmorrage one day after Nick's birth.

But there were happy things to talk about as well. The Cosgroves' son-in-law wasn't an unknown golf pro anymore. In June of 1952, Julius Boros (known to his friends as Jay) won the U.S. Open, beating Ben Hogan, Sam Snead and Jimmy Demaret at Northwood Club in Dallas.

"Look, Peggy, if you want to get into the golf business, I have an idea," Cosgrove said. "You remember Pine Needles, across the street from us? It's been owned by the Catholic Church for five years. They don't want to run the golf course any more. The course is for sale— $50,000 is the price. Let's get Jay and the five of us go in together and buy it. Bullet can run it while you're playing golf."

It didn't take the young couple long to decide to do it. The newly-weds pooled their resources, including Peggy's sale of some property she'd inherited in Findlay, and put up $20,000 for Pine Needles. The Cosgroves put up $15,000 and Boros, the pro tour's leading money-winner in 1952 with just over $37,000, put up $15,000.

The golf course they bought was in bad shape. Most of the grass on the fairways was dead. Rain had cut ruts all over the course. The greens were patchy and bumpy.

The golf course came with a five-year lease on a clubhouse that stood beside the original first tee (today the eighteenth) as well as barracks built by the Army Air Force that stood a hundred yards or so away. Today the barracks are gone, but the clubhouse building remains (you can see it to the left of the first fairway, about a hundred yards from the green) and is used as administrative offices for St. Joseph of the Pines. "The Golfery," as the barracks was called, could hold about fifty men, paying fifteen dollars a day for room, board and golf, but there was no hot water at first.

Weekends were the busy times, when golfers would board a train in New York City after work Thursday, travel all night and be met by the Bells in one of their two station wagons at the Southern Pines depot at seven o'clock Friday morning. The guests played golf all day Friday, Saturday and Sunday and would gather around the dinner table each evening for a family-style meal. The Bells served an early dinner on Sunday and put them on the train at seven-thirty Sunday night, back to New York in time for work Monday morning.

"It wasn't fancy," Peggy says. "We'd pick them up in a station wagon next to the big buses from the Carolina Hotel, taking other people to Pinehurst."

"Thank goodness our guests stuck by us," said Bullet. "We were always the last resort in the area to fill up for the season, but our friends kept coming back. Thanks to them, we kept Pine Needles alive."

Meanwhile, Homeland Investment Company of Durham continued to own Mid Pines, as it had since 1934. But by the mid-1950s, it wanted out of the resort business and offered the resort to the Cosgroves, the long-time managers. In order for the Cosgroves to raise the necessary funds to buy the resort, they had to get their cash by selling out of Pine Needles. They wanted $60,000 from the Bells to buy out their interest as well as Boros's share.

"But you only put $30,000 into it two years ago," Bullet said.

"I know," Maisie said. "But that's what we've got to have. And we've got someone who'll pay it."

Caught on short notice, the proud young couple was forced to do something it never wanted to do—borrow from Peggy's father. Robert Kirk had tried time and time again to interest the young couple in moving to Findlay and taking over his wholesale grocery business. And now he tried once more.

But their hearts were in golf.

"If your mind is made up, I'll help you," he said.

The Bells ran the resort for two more years before their desperate search for money to build their first lodges. They conquered that one, thanks to a couple of savvy insurance men. But that wasn't the only hurdle they'd have to leap. The next year, they still had no clubhouse. Bullet drew the plans during the summer of 1958 and hired a contractor to build a clubhouse and dining room. Then, when the contractor raised his price, Bullet said, "We'll build it ourselves."

Their lease had expired on the "Golfery" June 1st and they had reservations for golfers beginning November 1st. By mid-August, the clubhouse was running over budget and they were out of money to finish and furnish it.

"What do we do now?" Bullet wondered.

"I've got an idea," Peggy said.

She drove to Pinehurst to the Carolina Bank, which had operated since 1914 (originally it was the Bank of Pinehurst). The bank served the employees and guests of Pinehurst Inc. as well as the village cottagers. And though it was independent from Pinehurst Inc., Richard Tufts was the bank president. Would the bank loan money to another golf resort, one that in theory could be competing for the same guests? "The bank gave us the money we needed and then some more," Peggy says. "They said they didn't consider us competition and thought any growth was good for the area. It was a wonderful gesture."

The money in hand, it was still a race to the opening of the season to finish the building. Bullet bet carpenters steak dinners they couldn't finish various parts by certain times. The work moved quickly. When guests arrived in early November, they sat on one side of the dining room while hammers pounded and kitchen equipment was installed. The guests even helped unpack furniture. By November third, the clubhouse was finished.

The 1958-59 season dawned with the Bells owning their entire facility—twenty rooms, clubhouse, dining room and golf course. Now they set about expanding each year with profits from the previous season and more money from the Carolina Bank. Along the way, they were innovators. "We were the first golf course in the area to have golf carts," Peggy says. "Richard Tufts swore there'd never be a golf cart in Pinehurst. But we'd been to Florida. We'd seen what was happening. We were the first hotel in the area to have air conditioning. We had the first swimming pool in the area."

As the Bell family grew (Bonnie was born in 1954, followed by Peggy Ann in 1958 and Kirk in 1962), so too did Pine Needles. The resort always reflected the personality of its owners.

"Pine Needles represents Peggy so well," Ann Casey Johnstone says. "It's classy but casual. Classy but casual. That's Peggy Kirk Bell."

The kids stuffed envelopes and hand-addressed them for a dime a day. "I'm sure it looked good to get something hand-addressed by a twelve-year-old," Bonnie says. In the summers, the resort closed down, and the family would take its reservation records to the pool, where they'd field inquiries for the coming season while honing their swimming and diving abilities.

Peggy liked action—whether it was flying her plane, driving fast or scooting around the golf course or Southern Pines on one of the two motorcycles given to her by Bill France Jr., who befriended the Bells while staying at Pine Needles during the construction of North Carolina Motor Speedway in Rockingham, half an hour down the road.

Peggy and Bullet take the family for a ride in their new golf cart in the early 1960s. Peggy's holding Peggy Ann, while Kirk and Bonnie hang on in the back. Pine Needles had the Sandhills area's first golf carts.

Peggy Ann turned crimson the day her mother drove up on a Yamaha 100 to her middle school to pick her up. "Mom, I'll walk around the corner to the church," the little girl said. "You pick me up there." Peggy gave the cycles away when Kirk showed an interest in learning to ride.

While the kids helped where they could and Peggy provided the famous name, the warm smile and the expertise on the lesson tee, Bullet was the glue that held the resort together from a business and logistical perspective. Bullet's father died when he was young and he and his brother Russell grew up in modest surroundings. He never took anything for granted; part of the motivation for working long hours was that he wanted better for his children. He was also quick to help others who needed a break. Hundreds of young amateurs stayed at Pine Needles over the years at no charge while playing in local tournaments, including the North and South Amateur, and dozens of struggling young pros stayed there when the PGA Tour was making its regular stops at Pinehurst No. 2 in the 1970s. One of those was Pat McGowan, the eventual son-in-law who met Bonnie while staying at Pine Needles during the 1977 PGA Tour Qualifying School.

Bullet was never adverse to any job. He'd help cook breakfast, then tee golfers off the first tee, then help make beds. He sometimes cleaned late into the night to save money.

And if you second-guessed him or challenged his ability to accomplish something, beware. "You didn't tell him he couldn't do something," Bonnie says. "He would do it just to prove you wrong." He was as competitive in later years as he was as a youth on the basketball floor, and it aggravated him one year that he was losing frequently on the golf course to Peggy. While his wife was on the pro tour, Bullet took lessons and prepared eagerly for their matches upon her return. He shot a seventy-five and beat her by two shots.

Bell was an immaculate dresser. "At dinner we'd always wait to see what he was wearing," says Mary Davies, a long-time family friend and the wife of Bob Davies, a fellow early NBA player with Bell. "He was a sartorial dresser." He wore ultra-suede jackets, his shirt sleeves were monogrammed, and the cuffs of his trousers had to fall one-half inch from front to back. It was enough for son Kirk to joke with his dad that he was "like a girl getting ready for dinner." The kids remember the famous occasion of Bullet getting his ultra-suede slacks and jacket covered in grease and mud while driving a moped during a family vacation to Bermuda.

Bell was also renowned for his dry sense of humor and ability to give the needle. McGowan knew that a confident and nonchalant approach would be best with Bullet when broaching the subject of marriage to Bonnie, so he visited Bullet in his office one morning in 1981 and said, "I think you need a golf pro in the family, so would it be okay if I married Bonnie?"

Bullet looked over his glasses at the nervous young man. "You'd better ask her first," he said.

"You realize she'll take a pay cut if she marries you?" Bell said.

Though no official records are kept, doctors and hospital staffers marveled at Bell's ability to recover from major heart surgery in 1972. "He was out of the hospital and back at work in seven to ten days, and that was unheard of at the time," Peggy Ann says.

There was always another project, another tweaking of the resort to make things better for the guests—and in the long run, better for the family business.

"Bullet had great imagination," Mary Davies says. "The walkway from one end of the lodge to the other was so people could walk to dinner and not get wet if it was raining. He built the covered stalls on the driving range so they could hit balls without getting wet. I think the meeting room in the early-1970s was his final achievement. He seemed to have reached all of his goals with that."

Warren Bell died in 1984. Friends and family members remember that, beyond the excellent golf course and comfortable surroundings, what made Pine Needles a success was the hands-on involvement of the owners.

"Every night they'd visit with the guests in the dining room or in the bar after dinner," says Mary Davies. "How many places can you go where the owners will sit and talk with the guests?"

Bell once talked about contrasts of the demands on the family's time and the rewards of running a successful resort:

"You know why most resorts aren't operated by the owner? Few people want to work eighteen hours a day like Peg and I do.

"But I don't think we could be happy in any other business. It's not just the money. Like Peg's dad told us, there are a lot easier ways to earn a living.

"But it is golf, and that is an important thing with both of us. I love it even when Peg beats me." ∎

CHAPTER FOUR

THE GENIUS
OF DONALD ROSS

If you can't go to Dornoch, a day's travel across the Atlantic to London and then Edinburgh, with four difficult hours by auto up road A9 to the northeast peninsula of Scotland, through kilt and bagpipe country dotted with sheep and whitewashed farmhouses, where it doesn't get dark in June until midnight; if you can't play the ancient links course there, Royal Dornoch Golf Club, overlooking the Dornoch Firth and the North Sea, where one Donald James Ross learned the game of golf, where a caddie named Sandy Matheson might advise prior to a delicate putt, "Now ya must just tickle her, sir;" if you can't don your tweed cap and cardigan and go round and round and round a treeless golf course punctuated by wind, devilish bunkers and thick, ornery bushes called whins; and if you can't relax with a tumbler of The Macallan single malt whisky and a plate of haggis and bed down in a castle that's over eight hundred years old ....

Then you certainly can visit Southern Pines, North Carolina, where two of Ross's most venerable old golf courses sit nestled in the sandy loam, pine straw and wire grass, much like they did some seventy years ago. And that's exactly what eighty-nine members of the Donald Ross Society have done this weekend in the spring of 1995.

Over three days, they played golf at Pine Needles Lodge & Golf Club and across Midland Road at Mid Pines Inn & Golf Club. They marveled at the contrasts of Ross's design handiwork—the apparent simplicity of the holes as viewed by the naked eye and their confounding complexity as you try to place drives, hit approach shots tight, get little chip shots

Mid Pines and Pine Needles designer Donald Ross in 1922.

TUFTS ARCHIVES/COURTESY ELIZABETH SHAPIRO

close to the hole and, blast it, make a few birdies. They enjoyed the fellowship in the home up the road a bit, alongside the third green of the No. 2 course at Pinehurst Resort & Country Club, where Ross lived from 1925 until his death in 1948.

And they pledged allegiance to what Ross meant to golf—and still does.

George Burke is hitting balls on the practice tee at Pine Needles as the shadows cast by the towering pines in the late afternoon sun creep across the driving range. Burke, a four-handicapper from Salem Country Club in Peabody, Massachusetts, is one of the original members of the Ross Society. The group was formed in 1988 by four members of a Ross course in the throes of a hangover after seeing what a modern architect had wrought in the name of "updating" their classic course.

"You've got more traditional golf here than anywhere in the country," Burke says. "If you can't get to Dornoch, and believe me, it's a long, hard haul, you can almost feel like you're in Dornoch right here. This is where a lot of golf began in this country. It's been kept alive though the years. You come here and you feel like you're a part of it. You notice some of the guys from the big cities—New York, Boston, Chicago, they're used to going fast and moving at a quicker pace—they come here and they slow down. They take it easy."

Burke pauses and looks to his left, where the first hole of the Pine Needles course runs up a gentle slope beyond a row of pine trees.

"You can stand on the first tee and imagine it's been like this forever," he says. "Sure, the buildings around the range are new. The trees are taller. But other than that, it's all here. You can see Donald Ross was here. His hand is in the trees, in the ground."

He goes on, hitting balls, pausing now and then to talk about the lure of a Ross course—"If you've got one you've one of the true gems," he says; about the playability of his courses—"I'm a four-handicap, the guy I'm traveling with is a twelve or thirteen. We can go to the tiger tees and neither one of us is overwhelmed."

And about the importance of preserving and protecting these relics.

"I think there's a feeling in most all facets of life today—let's hold on to the past, let's not rush forward so fast," Burke says, then turns back to hit some more golf balls.

* * *

Imagine a twenty-seven-year-old chucking a bright career, one securely founded with instruction under the masters of his trade at the finest outlets for learning in existence.

Imagine leaving this to go to a country he knew little about, where he had only one casual acquaintance, with hardly any money, where his industry was merely an infant with no guarantees of growing or prospering.

Do that and you'll have in a feathery the daunting risk assumed by Donald Ross in 1899 as he boarded a boat for New York and a new life as an American golf professional.

But Ross had faith in a game that had mesmerized and captivated his Scottish ancestors for nearly five centuries. He believed the golf bug would bite and suck and consume the American—just give it a little time.

"When I was a young man in Scotland, I read about America and that the American businessman was absorbed in making money," Ross said. "I knew that the day would come when the American businessman would relax and want some game to play, and I knew that game would be golf. I read about the start of golf in the United States and I knew there would be a great future in it. I learned all I could about the game: teaching, clubmaking, greenkeeping, golf-course construction and came to grow up with a game in which I had complete confidence."

Ross's early days have been well-documented: Born in 1872 in Dornoch to working-class parents; exposed to golf as a youngster as a caddie and player at Royal Dornoch; later a teen-aged employee of the green crew at Dornoch; apprenticed as a greenkeeper and clubmaker under Old Tom Morris at St. Andrews and in Robert Forgan's clubmaking shop; hired at twenty years of age as head professional and greenkeeper at Dornoch.

Ross developed an early interest in the fundamentals of course design and an appreciation for the strategy and beauty of the surroundings inherent in the courses at St. Andrews and Royal Dornoch. Morris was the greenkeeper at St. Andrews from 1864 for nearly forty years and, in 1886, revised Dornoch into its present layout. Upon returning to Dornoch, young Ross and another mentor, Royal Dornoch club secretary John Sutherland, spent hours wandering the links, discussing shot values and making subtle changes here and there to Morris's holes.

The popular belief is that Ross accepted a formal invitation to come to America from a Harvard professor named Robert Willson, who had visited Dornoch in 1899 (and the popular spelling of "Wilson" is incorrect, according to Ross historian Pete Jones of Raleigh, North Carolina).

Construction methods were primitive in the 1920s when Mid Pines and Pine Needles were built, with Donald Ross having at his disposal only mules, men and drag pans to move earth. The result was holes like the one shown on succeeding pages – the 12th at Pine Needles that is now the 11th.

In fact, Willson was impressed by Ross's ability as a teacher and for a tip on finding a good tailor in Dornoch. In fact, Willson suggested to Ross that golf was new and growing in America, that Ross ought to visit and, if he did, look him up. But there were no prior arrangements made and no job set up in advance.

Nevertheless, Willson did provide Ross a sandwich and a glass of milk late upon the evening of Ross's arrival late in 1899—after an eight-mile hike through snow from the train station to Willson's home (Ross didn't understand Willson's telephone-dictated instructions on how to find a trolley). And Willson did help him find work at Oakley Country Club.

When Ross first came to America, his mission was to teach the game. But he was quick to note golf courses that could be improved with bunkers added or moved for strategic intrigue or shot-making challenge, with greens and tees repositioned, with the land better used to provide options and risks-and-rewards. He knew that if golf were to thrive in America, more courses needed to be built. So he was eager to take on design projects around the Boston area, often at little or no fee.

No skilled labor was available for construction, so Ross had to direct each man. "Imagine, if you can, a contractor employed to build a house, who can find no workmen who have ever worked on a house before, and you will have some idea of what it meant to be the first golf architect in America," an early newspaper account said.

One of the students in Ross's early golf schools at Oakley was a lawyer who had a client named James Tufts, the founder of the Pinehurst resort in the Sandhills of North Carolina. By the fall of 1900, Tufts had eighteen holes at Pinehurst, laid out by himself with assistance from Dr. D. Leroy Culver and/or George C. Dutton, depending on which edition of the *Pinehurst Outlook* you might happen across. There was some disagreement between Tufts and his son, Leonard, over whether golf was a fad or a sport for the ages, but nonetheless they believed Pinehurst's golf inventory needed expansion, and they needed an experienced director of the operation for the late fall, winter and early spring seasons. Tufts invited Ross to his home for an interview and, at the end of the meeting, had agreed to hire Ross.

Ross arrived in Pinehurst on December 7th, 1900, and shot an eighty on his first inspection of the Pinehurst course. He was immediately struck by the similarity between the sandy ground at Pinehurst and that of his native Scotland. The terrain at the time was basically treeless as

well—just like the windswept landscapes of St. Andrews and Dornoch.
He set about his myriad of responsibilities—teaching the game, making clubs, shepherding the guests around the courses, supervising the caddies, administering tournaments created to generate publicity for the resort. What he enjoyed the most, though, was designing new golf holes. He built nine for the No. 2 course by 1903, then a full eighteen by 1907. No. 3 opened in 1910, No. 4 in 1919.
By 1910, he was a golf course architect full time.

* * *

It hurts Dick Cesana just to think about it. The six-handicapper at Metacomet Country Club, a 1921 Ross creation in East Providence, Rhode Island, shakes his head while relaxing with a post-round libation in the bar at Pine Needles, overlooking the putting green and the first tee.

"Three guys didn't like the way the seventh green was situated," he says. "It was a downhill par-three with a wonderful view of Watchemoket Cove in the distance. These guys didn't like having to walk up a hill from the seventh green to the eighth tee. They wanted the green raised. They were in the insurance business. So they told the superintendent, 'We'll each give you a life insurance policy if you'll rebuild the hole.' "

So the hole was rebuilt. The green was raised, taking away the dramatic view, and the third hole, which skirted the seventh green to the right, was affected as well.

"It was a crime. It makes you want to cry," Cesana says.

This was in 1951. Over time, other changes were made to the course. Today, Cesana is spearheading the effort to restore Metacomet to Ross's original design—and fortunately, the club has all of his drawings. Once the work is finished, it will take a change in the club's by-laws to change the golf course. It's been a challenge, Cesana admits, with interclub politics being what they are. But the result will be worth it to this man who credits the Ross Society with changing the way he looks at a golf course.

"This group has opened up a whole new world," he says. "Now I look at golf courses like I never did before. I've played golf for thirty-five years and it's only been the last five or six I've paid any attention to the design of a golf course, to why someone did this or did that or put that here.

"Ross courses, you can play them all your life. They aren't penal. If you get into trouble, you're probably going to lose a half a shot. It's not so discouraging. You're not constantly fighting fires. He's got those

91

Ross (second from right) on old third at Pine Needles (current second).

subtle rolls in his greens, but not the dramatic fall-offs you see in some modern greens."

Through the knowledge and contacts Cesana has made through the Ross Society, he found a golf architect with a profound appreciation for the classics and Ross to supervise the renovation at Metacomet. Ron Prichard, a golf architect headquartered outside Philadelphia, says some of the changes made to old courses are like spray painting the Sistine Chapel. And that playing many new courses is a brutal affair for average golfers.

"Today the fashion is a very penal style of design," says Prichard. "The men and women who play golf as a hobby visit these modern courses and struggle through a round where their spirit is gradually broken. That is not the purpose of the Royal and Ancient game, and to experience the difference one simply has to step on a course designed by Ross."

* * *

Donald Ross is known for the four hundred, sixteen golf courses his company, Donald Ross Associates, designed over his forty-eight years in America and the many more it remodeled or had built from plans only (add the two numbers together and you get the six hundred-plus courses he's often credited with). But Ross's contributions to the game were many more and, despite the crunch on his time and his design business, he was still able to live a varied and rich life.

Ross gave America its first golf school, one of the first dedicated practice ranges, early research on speed of play, development of grass greens in North Carolina, and the first golf course designed with ladies in mind.

Ross established an indoor golf school during his first winter in Boston, in 1900, when Oakley Country Club was closed. He devised the driving nets and soon had a large group of golfers interested in learning the methods of the great Scottish players.

He took his forum for teaching the game to the next logical step several years later by dedicating some acreage where some holes of the old No. 1 course at Pinehurst existed and making it a practice range. The accepted form of teaching until that time was the playing lesson, but golfers in 1913 could now experiment with shot after shot without slowing down players behind them on the course. The practice tee was soon dubbed "Maniac Hill."

In the early 1920s, Ross was troubled over the speed of play at the four courses at Pinehurst Country Club. He sent his seven assistants out for three weeks during the spring of 1921 to time matches on all four golf courses at Pinehurst. The result was a timetable that projected where each match should be at certain intervals—perhaps a forerunner to the USGA's time/par system.

The ideal time for eighteen holes? Two hours and forty minutes.

Ross concluded that "any four-ball match which wastes no time between strokes nor on the green or between the last putt on one green and the first drive on the next is able to complete the circuit in entire comfort in two hours and forty minutes."

The timetable published in the *Pinehurst Outlook* directed golfers to "take plenty of time playing shots. Walk smartly between shots."

(No doubt considerable time was saved on the greens during this era. The greens at Pinehurst were made of a sand/clay base and dusted with sand on the top to help reduce the speed of putts. All greens were flat, so there was little time wasted looking at putts from four angles to gauge break and grain.)

Ross always coveted grass greens for his courses at Pinehurst, Mid Pines, Pine Needles and Southern Pines Golf Club, rather than the original sand/clay bases, but he was afraid that the grass greens already developed in the deep south would be killed at the first frost as far north as the Sandhills. He and course superintendent Frank Maples began experimenting with a strain of rye grass in the early 1930s on a developmental green near the No. 2 course. Ross covered it on cold nights.

"One night he missed covering it and found in the morning that the frost had not hurt the grass," said Richard Tufts, president of Pinehurst Inc. from 1935-62. "He was one very happy man that day."

Pinehurst No. 3 was the first course ever designed with ladies in mind. The layout, located on the west side of Hwy. 5, opened in 1913 at a length of 6,284 yards. Hazards were placed to fit a woman's ball- flight, and the course became the site of the annual North and South Women's Amateur.

All the while, Ross was able to maintain an excellent game himself (he shot a sixty-six at age sixty-two on No. 3); he demanded the high standards for clubmaking he'd learned at St. Andrews (he'd take any new woods he acquired to the repair shop and meticulously shave the faces to open the clubface a wee bit); and he still found time to cultivate a rose garden, observe afternoon tea and take an active interest in building the Village Chapel in Pinehurst.

And he lived with a refreshing perspective on life and the role golf played in it, which he shared with a Rochester, New York, newspaperman during an interview in 1947, just a year before his death.

"These young fellows are so completely wrapped up in getting a little golf ball into a little hole in less strokes than anyone else that their attitude and sense of intelligent balance to the more important things in life is not only distorted but practically non-existent," Ross said.

"These boys acquire the idea that golf, or tennis, for that matter, is terribly, terribly, important. They read about themselves in the sporting pages and they become complacent and eager for more and greater laurels.

"What is happening is that you cannot carry on an intelligent conversation with most of these big-name youngsters. Sooner or later, the talk backfires to golf. Now golf is a fine game. I would be the last man to say it wasn't. It has been my relaxation and livelihood ever since I was a little shaver in Scotland.

"But, when the game of golf becomes so all-important, and feverish, and holier than anything else in life, then parents might do worse than turn their young careerists over their knees and administer an old-fashioned spanking."

* * *

Steve Kircher grew up in an environment steeped in the traditions of golf. His father, Everett, is an eminent ski and golf developer in northwest Michigan, having opened Boyne Mountain in 1947 and Boyne Highlands in 1963. He also was a frequent visitor to Pinehurst and an aficionado of Ross's work. In the late-eighties, the elder Kircher seeded the idea of building a golf course with holes patterned after great ones from Ross courses such as Pinehurst No. 2, Seminole, Oak Hill, Oakland Hills, Royal Dornoch and Salem.

The result, the Donald Ross Memorial, opened with nine holes in 1989 and a full eighteen in 1990.

Kircher is standing in the pine forest behind the home of Wayne and Jo Ashby, who bought the old Ross home when they moved to Pinehurst in 1989. Each year, the Ross Society visits for a cocktail buffet. Kircher, a scratch-handicapper, nods towards the third green of the No. 2 course.

"In the mid-eighties, Jack Nicklaus had just opened a new course in our area," he says, referring to The Bear at Grand Traverse Resort. "It was the antithesis of what this is. No one seemed to remember who Donald Ross was at the time. Something was wrong. If Nicklaus could do something like that, get all this p.r. and have people talking about it, people had totally lost touch with the way the game was. We said, 'We need to do something to bring the game back.'

"Gradually, the pendulum has come back. People are tired of penal designs. The Ross Society was formed. The Ross Memorial opened. Crystal Downs (an Alister Mackenzie antique that opened in 1932) started getting some recognition. And on and on and on. Now we're back to where we're supposed to be. No. 2 is back in the top ten. It's all good. There's so much heart and soul in the game. You can't lose it."

Kircher arrived in Southern Pines the afternoon before and scooted out as fast as possible for nine holes at Mid Pines. His game is rusty, having come from the shores of Lake Michigan where skiing is still possible in mid-April, but even bogeys couldn't dampen his enthusiasm as he studied every detail of the golf course.

"If you take so much of finesse game out of it, all it becomes is power" he says. "Target, target, target, target, target. Ross really understood the concept of all the clubs in the bag, all the different shots, all the different touch, feel type things. When you play his courses, it puts so much pressure on your short game, on your long game, on your ability to think. It moves you back in the fairway knowing you've got to hit a certain point. For a good player, there's a lot going on, even though it looks simple. It's downright great architecture."

* * *

The design of golf courses at the turn of the century in America was an unscientific process. One early design school consisted of laying eighteen stakes on a Sunday afternoon and getting twenty-five dollars for the effort.

Donald Ross changed all of that. And the golf-course design industry has him to thank today. "He's one of the premier golf course architects of the golden age of golf courses," says Tom Fazio. "As many golf courses as were created in the late-eighties and nineties, many more were done in the Roaring Twenties. The quality and playability of his courses stand out in my mind. And he was responsible more than anyone else for making golf-course architecture a profession."

Adds Pete Dye: "He was one of the very few designers who were able to put a real purpose into each shot on every hole."

Ross's designs were predicated on using the natural flow of the land to dictate the routing, on instituting as much thinking as swinging into the game and to demand a player be adept at every kind of shot. He particularly believed that chipping in a variety of circumstances and the ability to hit long irons were the true measuring sticks of quality players. And he didn't like water; he believed the loss of two shots was too severe. The two courses that most molded Ross's design philosophy, Royal Dornoch and St. Andrews, are affected by water mostly from the wind whipping off the sea.

His first step in evaluating any site was to pick eighteen natural sites for greens. Other parts of a course could be manufactured if needed, but the green sites had to come with the ground. He left the greatest margin for error on the longest shot, the tee shot, and drew the fairways in tighter where the shots of longer hitters were likely to land. There was always plenty of room for the average player to hit, but for good players, there was always a specific point in the fairway that afforded the best angle of approach into the green.

On the eighth at Pine Needles, for example, it's always important to drive to the left side of the fairway; if the flag's on the left side of the green on number twelve or eighteen, you need to approach from the right side. The sixth fairway has a crown in the landing area, and it's helpful to hit your approach from the top of the crown, where you have a level lie, than going fifteen yards farther and having a downhill lie. "I'll often hit a three-wood off the sixth tee to make sure I don't roll down the slope," says Kelly Miller, general manager of Pine Needles and a prominent Carolinas amateur golfer.

Ross's career might well have still evolved toward architecture had he remained a club professional in the Boston area. But certainly his position in Pinehurst offered a form of advertising unique in his business. Golfers came from all around the country and, by 1919, all seventy-two holes at Pinehurst Country Club were his. "Come build us a course in Detroit," a visitor would say. Or Rochester. Or Chicago. Or Connecticut. By 1910, Ross was a designer first and foremost and left the rest of the golf operations to his assistants. So prolific was his work in the first quarter of the century that six of eight national Opens from 1919 and 1926 were played on Ross courses.

Over time, a sense of what makes a Ross course so special evolved:

* You can figure out how to play every hole from the tee.

* The fairway landing areas are wide at first glance but, upon closer inspection, offer one prime location for the best angle-of-approach to the flag.

* Greenside bunkers are often placed ten to twenty yards in front of the putting surfaces. The popular notion today is that Ross placed them there to create an "optical illusion," to play havoc with your depth perception and lure you into thinking the green is closer than it really is. While that is certainly an effect of the design, Ross's real intent in a day when golf was more of a ground game than an air game was to provide room for a shot to clear the bunker but still land in front of the green and roll up.

* Greens in sandy soils like those in Southern Pines and Pinehurst are surrounded by mounds and hollows, requiring imaginative chips and pitches.

* Fairway bunkers are often placed on the side of the fairway that affords the best approach to the green.

* There will be five to six holes (with at least one of them being a par-three), requiring a long-iron approach to the green.

* There will also be a short par-three and a short par-four, each with a small, well-guarded green with more undulations than most.

* Bunkers have faces bulging from top to bottom, with sand flashed onto the front bank. Authentic Ross bunkers also have concave floors instead of flat ones, facilitating shots landing in bunkers to settle near the center instead of under the face and to improve drainage.

Ross's work spanned several eras, from the beginning when greens were made of sand and clay and when primitive implements were used to move earth. Later, greens were covered with grass, and tractors made shaping easier. When he came to America, golfers rarely carried more than six clubs in the their bags. By the mid-1930s, innovative clubmakers had created a club for every situation; Lawson Little had thirty clubs in his bag in the 1937 North and South Open. The next year, the fourteen-club limit was instituted. But Ross courses always have a seamless quality that was never spoiled by developments in technology.

"Ross courses are generally more of a second-shot course," says David Eger, a veteran golf administrator with the USGA and PGA Tour. "And you usually run through the entire bag of clubs by the tenth or eleventh hole. More than anything, you've got to think on every shot, every hole."

Ross didn't personally supervise every job, which led to some regrets in his later years. He had two full-time supervisors, Walter Hatch and J.B. McGovern, and an engineer, Walter Irving Johnson. In his heyday in the 1920s, Ross employed as many as eight construction superintendents and three thousand workers. Some of his courses were designed by mailing back a routing on a topographical map, which could lead to the kind of snafu he encountered with a course in the Canadian Rockies in 1910. Ross designed the course on paper, but his client refused to pay Ross his requested thirty-five dollars-a-day rate to come supervise construction. Ross used inches to measure contours on greens and in bunkers, but the Canadian construction chiefs interpreted them as feet—leading to greens with twelve-foot rolls and bunkers twenty feet deep. The mistake wasn't discovered until nine holes had been built.

"It bothered him that golf courses listed his name as the designer and he'd never stepped foot on the property," says Peter Tufts, great-grandson of Pinehurst founder James Tufts and Ross's godchild.

Nonetheless, any Ross course today is a special one—provided it's not been chopped beyond recognition by green committees or heavy-handed modern designers.

"Any club owning a Donald Ross course should jealously protect what they have," said Richard Tufts, Peter's father. "The owner of a Rembrandt painting would hardly turn it over to an impressionist painter for modernization."

Tom Fazio was asked in the spring of 1995 by a filmmaker working on a centennial documentary on Pinehurst what Ross would be doing if he were still alive.

"I would think that Donald Ross would have a staff of people answering the telephones because there'd be so many people calling him to design golf courses," Fazio said. "And the rest of us in the industry would be fighting for number two position as best we could."

* * *

At last count, Michael Fay had played one hundred and five Donald Ross golf courses. One of the four founding members of the Donald Ross Society, Fay has an established insurance agency in Connecticut that allows him the freedom to play a lot of golf. He goes out of his way to find Ross courses he's never seen. Often he'll play alone at daybreak and provide evaluations for club officials covering what looks authentic in the design of the course versus what's the creation of assorted members over the years. He enjoys the public courses as much as private ones, noting that a course such as George Wright Municipal in Boston is pretty much still as it was upon opening in 1931. "Being a municipal course, they haven't had the money to screw it up," Fay says.

"The golf courses are a work of art," he says. "Even though they're living, breathing things, it's a nice thought that you can play the same ground today and come back in fifty years with your great grandson and it will be the same. You have a basis for comparison. Plain and simple, they just don't build golf courses like this anymore.

"I don't want to knock modern architects. I really and truly enjoy modern courses. Four of my favorite twenty are Pete Dye courses. (Tom) Weiskopf and (Jay) Morrish have done great work. There's a place for new golf-course architecture. But I have a real hard time putting a classic course in the hands of a journeyman architect who butchers the work of a master."

Fay notes that Pine Needles was where Ross played most of his golf the last ten to fifteen years or so of his life. "He could no longer handle No. 2," he says. He marvels over his round that afternoon at Mid Pines; the old track yielded nothing easy to a good player.

"I love the give-and-take you find on courses like these, the back and fourth," he says. "At Mid Pines, for example, you've got the long, difficult, uphill tenth. That's a hard par five. Then you've got the easily accessible fifteenth (a much shorter par-five). You've got a 150-yard par-three and a 231-yard par-three. It goes back and forth. You get a little break here.

"Take a short hole like fourteen. You can hit an iron off the tee and you've got a nasty little sucker of a green to deal with. How many courses do you know play 6,400 yards and can be as difficult as that one? My longest approach today was a seven-iron on eighteen. I'm a scratch. And I didn't make one birdie."

* * *

Consider the case of one mid-handicapper and his family playing Mid Pines one idyllic afternoon in March 1994, and a Pine Needles course across the street full of serious, talented amateurs from around the state of North Carolina.

Bill Malouin and his wife, Linda, and son, Nicky, visited the Pinehurst area from Toronto for a week of golf and settled on Mid Pines, partly because Malouin liked the mature look of the course and because it wasn't too penal for his wife or son, both of whom essentially are beginners.

"There's really been no reason to go anywhere else," Malouin says. "It's a forgiving course. It's good for Nicky and Linda. There's no water to speak of, and it's hard to lose a ball."

Meanwhile, one hundred and twenty scratch handicappers are wrestling with Pine Needles in the second round of the inaugural North Carolina Mid-Amateur. Only two are under par through thirty-six holes.

"I love these old courses," says Lex Alexander, a former teaching pro under Claude Harmon at Winged Foot who owns a chain of grocery stores in Durham, North Carolina. "There's room to drive the ball. The greens are small. If you miss one, there are all these little humps and bumps to deal with. It's like a time warp."

And it's like Donald Ross said back in 1921, when he completed the Mid Pines course:

"Most golfers want to strike a happy medium of tastes. Wagner and Bach may be over-difficult for them to appreciate, and modern jazz may be too shallow for them to respond to. But opera and Viennese waltzes ... that's better."

Both the Mid Pines and Pine Needles courses (the latter was completed in 1928) sit today very much as they did when they first opened. The greens are now bentgrass, of course, after being converted from a sand/clay base to bermuda in the late 1930s, and the trees are much taller and thicker. The green on the ninth hole at Mid Pines was rebuilt and flattened by a previous owner several years ago, and to the seasoned observer stands out like yellow polyester slacks would on today's pro golf tour.

The holes at Mid Pines are still in their same positions and play only a little bit longer—the course opened at 6,393 yards and now is 6,515. There's a little more water on the course than there was originally; the pond in front of the third tee, for example, was built by long-time owner Frank Cosgrove for irrigation purposes. Meanwhile, little has been changed at Pine Needles with the exception that the St. Joseph of the Pines building was the original Pine Needles Inn and the first, ninth, tenth and eighteenth holes connected at the top of the hill on which the building still sits. The current eighteenth was once the first hole, the current eighth was the ninth, the current ninth was the tenth, and the current seventeenth was the eighteenth. That's why the halfway house

Two challenging par-threes Ross designed include the fifth at Pine Needles (top), a 207-yard carry across a valley, and the second at Mid Pines, 178-yard uphill shot that's particularly difficult when the hole's located on the right side of the green.

seems oddly positioned today at the ninth tee. The course opened at 6,436 yards and played at 6,708 before a 2004 restoration.

Happily, much of the strategic intrigue and Ross's shot values remain intact.

There isn't much lipstick and mascara on these courses. What there is, of course, is hundreds and hundreds of pine cones and thousands of pine needles, which to golf courses in these parts are like gumdrops on a gingerbread house. The needles are a golf hazard indigenous to this area; it's very difficult to play a shot off a lie of fluffy pine needles.

Mid Pines offers a suitable warm-up, with a downhill par-four of moderate length and a mid-iron par-three up next, and on the third hole begins taxing your course management and ability to control the ball. The third hole is dogleg right with woods through the fairway and a hazard right of the landing area, requiring tee shots hit to a precise length. The fourth is a tiny par-four of only 330 yards that sets up best with a tee shot hit from right-to-left, helping hold the severely canted fairway. Five is a reachable par-five, but a downhill lie from the green-light zone and a pond to the left of the fairway, about a hundred yards out, can combine for an equation like one-plus-one-equal-six.

Twelve is a strategic jewel, running 380 yards from right to left down the fairway. There's all the driving room in Moore County to the right side, but the angle is hideous into the green from that side. The hourglass shaped green is only nine paces across in the center and is flanked by a long bunker on the right side. If you position your drive on the left side of the fairway, the green is inviting, albeit still narrow. But there's a fairway bunker and woods on that side. So Ross's question is this: Do you play safe from the tee and have a harrowing approach; or do live dangerously off the tee in hopes of getting tight to the hole on your second?

Thirteen is a back-crunching par-three of 230 yards from the tips, while fourteen is a short two-shot hole with a fairway that throws everything to the right and a small, busy and well-bunkered green. The eighteenth at Mid Pines is one of the area's most picturesque finishing holes—a par-four of 411 yards, downhill off the tee, then up to the green framed in the rear by the stately Georgian-style hotel.

By the ninth hole at Pine Needles, you've probably used every club in the bag already. Driver, three-wood, wedge on the uphill, par-five opener; driver, two-iron on the 451-yard second; nine-iron on the delicate par-three third; six-iron to the fourth green, an uphill par-four; four-wood on the long par-three fifth; four- and five-irons into the sixth and seventh greens; seven- and eight-irons into the shorter eighth and ninth holes.

And if you miss any of the greens, the devil's in the details of how best to negotiate the little pitches and valleys in the green settings. They're admittedly not as dramatic as those around the greens of Pinehurst No. 2, but they're perplexing enough as you weigh the merits of a lob, a chip or a putt.

The par-threes at Pine Needles are particularly outstanding, ranging from the tiny third (134 yards downhill, across a pond); to the long fifth (208 yards across a chasm to the green); to the elegant thirteenth (surely one of the area's prettiest holes, 189 yards downhill). It finishes with a bang with the long, difficult eighteenth; the approach shot on this 426-yard hole is one of the harder ones on the course—a mid-iron off a hanging lie. Harold Williams, the long-time locker room attendant at Pine Needles who died in January 1995, was one of the few known to have driven within a few feet of the green.

"It's the kind of golf course you can't get bored with," says Brandie Burton, who won the USGA Girls Junior at Pine Needles in 1989. "Each hole has its own style. The greens are typical Donald Ross. They roll over on the ends. I love traditional golf courses. I feel really comfortable in that kind of atmosphere."

So do a number of other top pros who'll hope to vie for the Open championship.

"It's not that long, but it's tight, and the greens are going to be quick," says Jane Crafter, who once represented Pine Needles on the LPGA Tour. "There's plenty of trouble to get into. I think it will be a good course. I don't think it will be the hardest Open course ever played. But so what? It's about time the USGA let us play a course that's not totally impossible, where any mistake will cost you a couple of strokes."

"It's fun for me to play Donald Ross courses because they're so appealing to the eye," says Beth Daniel. "They're fair, they're not too tough. You won't pay a penalty with a triple if you hit a so-so shot. But they're still tough to score on. I much prefer the older courses to the new ones."

* * *

An article in "Golf Journal" previewing the USGA's 1987 championship venues described The Orchards Golf Club in South Hadley, Massachusetts, site of the United States Girls Junior, as "a fine old Donald Ross course." That caught Barry Palm's eye. Palm, at the time an advertising executive in Hartford, Connecticut, made a few telephone calls, and the day after the final round of the Girls Junior, Palm and

Ross came to America to carve his future in golf. He succeeded and brought much pleasure to many people–and still does.

three visitors from Wampanoag Country Club in West Hartford toured The Orchards.

Palm, Michael Fay, Bruce Taylor and Steve Edwards reveled in the charm of the quaint, New England village, the ivy-covered walls of Mount Holyoke College, the tall spire of the local church. The unpretentious club, Palm remembers, had "slamming screen doors and a great two-dollar hamburger." And also a wonderful old Ross course. By the second hole, a 350-yarder with a tiny green sloped severely from back to front, they knew they were traveling back in time.

"We were blown away by what a great golf course it was," Palm says, relaxing in Cosgroves Pub at Mid Pines, overlooking the eighteenth green. "It was pretty much intact with the original design. We fell in love with it."

They contrasted it with their own course, a 1924 Ross design that, unfortunately, had suffered at the hands of an egotistical president/green chairman and a heavy-handed modern architect. The former hooked the golf ball, and over the years removed fifty-three bunkers from the left sides of fairways and greens. "There was a tyrant in charge, an autocrat," Palm says. "He ruled with an iron fist." The latter rebuilt five green complexes in the mid-1980s without consulting Ross's original plans. "They were unsightly, unplayable and unmaintainable," Fay says. "And beside that, they fell apart."

As Palm walked off the eighteenth green at The Orchards that afternoon in 1987, he hatched the idea for the Donald Ross International Touring Society. The name was shortened, but the concept flourished. Today the society has more than twelve hundred members and has given $15,000 in scholarships to students of golf-course architecture; it has $70,000 in future scholarship funds in the bank.

Its mission above all: Create awareness among members of Ross courses that they are caretakers of classics; to proceed with caution before making changes; and to zealously protect what they have if their course is in its virgin state.

"All the members of this group share the same feeling about not only Donald Ross courses but other classic architects of that generation—Tillinghast, Mackenzie, Macdonald," says Palm, later executive director of the American Golf Sponsors Association in Ponte Vedra, Florida. "I hope if we've accomplished anything, people will think before doing something to one of these old golf courses. I hope we've raised a level of consciousness and sensitivity."

With that, it was time for Palm to go play golf—thirty-six holes a day for four straight days on courses that have changed little in three-quarters of a century. One certainly cannot get enough of Donald Ross. ∎

CHAPTER FIVE

THE TEACHING
TRADITION

T here was never any grand design on the part of Peggy and Warren Bell to turn their resort into a grass-ensconced university of golf. But it happened anyway—and quite by accident, by trial-and-error and by seizing opportunities.

The first milestone occurred in 1955 when a guest approached Bullet and asked if anyone taught golf lessons. Though the resort had no formal lesson structure, he figured that his wife, who competed at the upper echelons of the LPGA Tour, would certainly have something of value to tell the lady.

"That woman wants to learn to play golf," Bullet told Peggy. "Go teach her."

"I don't know what to tell her," Peggy said.

"You know more golf than she does. Tell her anything," Bullet said.

So the winner of the 1949 Titleholders Championship and member of the 1950 Curtis Cup team embarked on her first golf lesson. "And it was a disaster," Mrs. Bell says.

At the time, none of the present Pine Needles lodge or clubhouse facilities had been built. The Bells were operating out of two buildings near the original Pine Needles Inn, today the St. Joseph of the Pines nursing facility behind the current eighteenth and second tees (the first and third tees at the time). One of those buildings no longer exists, but the one used as a pro shop and dining room still stands, tucked in the woods to left of the first fairway as numbered today (it's used now

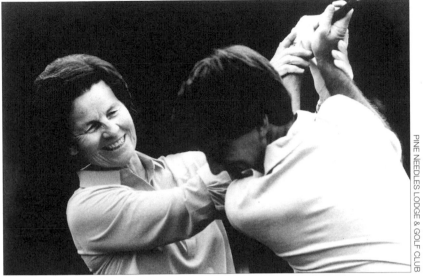

Peggy's hands-on teaching methods get golfers "in the spot."

as offices for St. Joseph). There was no practice area, just a small tee beside the pro shop, where up to three golfers could direct shots across the first fairway—pausing, of course, for passing golfers.

"That lesson was awful," Mrs. Bell says. "I told her everything I knew. We were out there for two or three hours. She'd hit it bad and I'd say, 'Try this.' Another bad shot. 'Try this.' I was going crazy trying to get her to hit it like I could.

"Finally, she said, 'Can we quit? I'm dead.' I would have stayed there until midnight. I often wonder about that poor woman. I'm sure she quit golf then and there."

That lesson piqued Peggy's interest in teaching, and she developed a close relationship with Ellen Griffin of the Woman's College of Greensboro (now UNC-G), a pioneer in women's golf instruction. The ladies were having lunch one day at Pine Needles in 1959 when Bullet bemoaned the fact that a business group, which had booked the entire resort for one week the following month, had just canceled.

"Bullet, let's put in a golf school for women," Ellen said.

"We can't do that, no one will come," Bell responded.

"Well, let's try."

"So we took out an ad in Golf World," Mrs. Bell remembers. "We charged $105 for four days and three nights. We had video equipment, which was a brand new thing then. We sent out mimeographed flyers

Many ads, like this one that ran in "Golf Digest" in 1970, touted Pine Needles
as the place where "Golf and and informality prevail."

to all the country clubs in North Carolina. We had fifty-three people
that first school."

That started the famed Peggy Kirk Bell "Golfari" tradition. Since
then, thousands of women golfers have learned the game at Pine Needles. So have men (they started men's golf schools in 1988). Couples,
families and youngsters have learned the game as well through an
assortment of Family and Youth Golfaris and through the annual Fellowship of Christian Athletes golf camp. Mrs. Bell has won numerous
awards in the world of golf instruction. She points to a shiny Rolex
wristwatch she received in 1989 for the Ellen Griffin Award for distinguished contributions to golf instruction.

"I was really proud to win that award," Mrs. Bell says. "She was
a big influence on my teaching career early. She knew there was a
vacuum of women teaching women."

The "Golfari" name was a take-off on "safari" and means a "week-
long excursion into golf." A full house of ladies, usually around a hundred and forty, generally arrive on Sunday afternoon during Golfari
weeks in February, May and September. Each day begins with a clinic
held by Peggy Bell and/or her son-in-law, former PGA Tour pro Pat
McGowan, followed by instruction, lunch and then golf in the afternoon. Following dinner, there's usually a golf movie or instruction
video. It's "gal's week out" with golf being the common thread.

Peggy admits she didn't know a lot about what she was doing at
first. One who helped her a great deal was Lee Kosten, a long-time

teaching pro whom she befriended while playing golf in Florida in the early 1950s. The Bells offered Kosten a job at Pine Needles in 1958. "I said, 'Lee, what am I going to tell them?' " Peggy says. "There wasn't a lot of teaching technique back then. You just taught the way you played.

"Lee said, 'You gotta get the grip right first. You can spend a whole lesson on the grip.' Then he sort of helped me with the takeaway and so forth. Why I felt so inadequate in teaching was that I'd never thought about anyone's game but my own. I think what everybody does is teach how they played. I had to have more than that.

"A lot of women would come to Pine Needles to take a lesson from a woman pro. Lee would come down and help me with them. I didn't feel qualified without him in the early days. When I'd get stuck with a lesson, I'd turn to Lee. We always taught side-by-side in the schools. I wanted him right by me."

At first, Peggy was nervous teaching men but later relaxed as she saw the results of emphasizing that power comes from a well-timed swing instead of hands and elbows flying and flailing and wrists snapping. Eventually, of course, she developed a style and flair for teaching all her own.

"Most of the success stories you never hear about," says Carol Johnson, a long-time friend and teaching pro. "The real success stories are taking a lady who shoots 160 and getting her to 100. Peggy gets a kick out of that."

"She can take any level you are and improve what you have, polish it up," says McGowan. "She loves helping people and gets as much satisfaction watching someone finally get it as that person does herself. She's as enthusiastic for the last lesson of the day as she is the first."

Pine Needles was the site every summer from the mid-1970s through the late-1980s of National Golf Foundation summer teaching seminars. At the time, education and instruction were important components of the NFG's program of work, and it held annual seminars at several sites around the country to show health and physical education instructors in public high schools how to teach golf and start golf programs in their schools. Staff instructors and guest speakers such as Conrad Rehling, DeDe Owens, Ellen Griffin, Jim Flick, Gary Wiren, Peter Kostis, Bob Rotella, Rod Myers, Dick Gordin, Bob Toski, Carol Johnson, Jim Suttie, Wally Armstrong and others attended over the years, imparting their wisdom to the physical education teachers to

Then And Now: Golfers are all ears when Peggy Kirk Bell teaches the golf swing, whether it's one-on-one in the 1960s (inset) or during a Golfari clinic in the early 2000s.

take back home and spread among the masses.

"Those seminars provided a tremendous amount of good to the game by spreading all of this teaching around the country," says Wiren.

"It was a very, very effective program for helping kids learn the basics about the game of golf," says Ed Cottrell, the former golf coach at Westchester State University who was program coordinator for the seminars at Pine Needles. "The slogan at the time for the seminars was, 'Those who dare to teach never cease to learn.'

"It was quite an incubator for ideas about teaching golf," Cottrell says. "And it was an ideal environment as well. I think the facility at Pine Needles is beyond anything I've seen. And Peggy had a rapport with everyone that was remarkable. She taught the golf swing the same way she swings a club herself—nice and relaxed and simple."

It was at these NGF seminars that Wiren hatched his idea for developing the "Laws, Principles and Preferences of the Golf Swing." By looking at the contrasting swings of golf greats such as the slashing Arnold Palmer and the syrupy Julius Boros, Wiren said, you could see there is no one perfect way to hit a golf ball. Instead, a teaching model could be developed that incorporated laws and principles (which would be standard among all golfers and teachers) with preferences (the act of choosing and liking a particular method or approach over another one). This model stands today as the cornerstone in many schools of teaching.

At one point in the late 1950s, before the Pine Needles teaching tradition had taken off, Bullet planned to dig up the swampy area where the driving range now sits and make it a lake.

"You'll be able to sit up in the dining room and look out over the lake," he enthused.

"But where will I teach?" Peggy asked.

Eventually, she won out. So Bullet decided if he had to lose his lake to a practice range, it had better be a good one. He built the practice shelters and installed mats so that instruction could continue in bad weather. He built a private teaching tee up on the hill to the right side of the range, beyond the last of the lodges.

Pine Needles never had any problem capturing and holding the women's market in golf instruction. It started Family Golfaris, usually held in late June, following by Youth Golfaris, usually held over the Fourth of the July week. Beginning in the late 1980s, it started paying more attention to the seemingly bottomless inventory of men wanting to learn to play better golf.

It held a men's golf school in March 1988, and continued with one a year for several more years. Then Pine Needles officials began planning for a state-of-the-art Learning Center that would be completed by the fall of 1992. When its doors were opened, the teaching staff had a classroom with all the modern conveniences and technology to teach men and women in small groups, no larger than sixteen and always with a four-to-one student-teacher ratio.

The 4,000-square foot facility is located at the far end of the driving range and has a two-bay indoor video station, seven sheltered practice stations, classroom space and an indoor putting green. It's loaded with gadgets and drills to help with everything from keeping elbows from flying to learning to hit off sidehill and downhill lies.

Today Pine Needles' golf schools are divided into the traditional Golfaris, held at specific dates, and Learning Centers, held throughout the year. Three-day Learning Centers run from Monday to Wednesday; four-day Learning Centers run from Thursday to Sunday. The Learning Centers are coordinated by McGowan and LPGA Tour pro Donna Andrews, Pine Needles' director of instruction, and augumented by additional expert instructors as needed.

"Creating a place for the men at Pine Needles was the next logical step," says McGowan. "You look at all the women coming over the years to Golfaris and you ask, 'Where are their husbands?'"

Pine Needles has developed a good following in its early years of targeting men, couples and small groups to visit its Learning Centers. The student-teacher ratio "makes it almost like taking a private lesson," as Walzak says, and McGowan's experience on the pro tour gives him a perspective in teaching course management that most teachers can't rival.

"The short game and course management are two areas that many golfers pay little attention to," McGowan says. "Too many golfers miss a fairway and try to hit a miraculous shot out of the trees and end up making a six or seven, when they should play back to safety, take a bogey and move on. Most golfers don't manage their way around the course very well.

"A lot of them are too worried about making the perfect swing and don't learn how to hit the little shots, the shots that can turn a bogey into a par. It's nice to have a great golf swing, but golf isn't only about swinging, it's also about scoring." ■

CHAPTER SIX

PEGGY'S PEARLS: TIPS FOR BETTER GOLF

P eggy Kirk Bell has given golf lessons to actors, CEOs, governors and golf pros. She's taught golf around the world, including a visit in early 1994 to India. She's won countless awards for instruction. She's penned dozens of instruction articles for *Golf Digest*, *GOLF* Magazine and *Golf World*. She's turned thirty-handicappers into scratch golfers (over time, of course).

So imagine her horror one day about thirty years ago when her golf instruction book rolled off the presses with a large photo of Mrs. Bell on the title page making a gangly and gruesome pass at a golf ball. Let's see: the club's past parallel at the top; the left wrist is cupped; the left heel is high in the air; the right elbow is flying; she's swayed too far to the right.

"I just about died when I saw that," Mrs. Bell says today. "The designers knew nothing about golf. They took a photo from the back of the book where I'm illustrating how not to swing. They said, 'It was the only picture of you swinging a club that showed your face.'"

A Woman's Way to Better Golf, by Mrs. Bell with Jerry Claussen, was a success nonetheless. Published in 1966, the book was marketed in the United Kingdom as well as the United States and provided the foundation to thousands of women who wanted to take up golf or improve their games.

Mrs. Bell has touched countless people through her book, her articles, her instructional videotape and, of course, through Pine

PINE NEEDLES LODGE & GOLF CLUB

Peggy Bell is a fixture in Sandhills and American golf teaching circles.

Needles' Golfaris, Learning Centers and private lessons. Some-one once said that teaching or coaching is saying the same thing, a thousand different ways. Mrs. Bell has certainly had some inventive ways to teach the golf swing over four-plus decades. Following are a sampling of the most helpful of "Peggy's Pearls."

Desire and Effort

So you want to be a good golfer. Well, you can. I've always be-lieved that becoming good in golf is less a matter of physical ability than it is in any other sport. Golf is only ten percent physical ability. The rest is mental, desire and effort.

When Mildred "Babe" Zaharias decided to become serious about golf, she quit playing with anyone for two years and instead hit a thou-sand golf balls a day. Admittedly, that's a bit extreme for most people. But you get the point. You can practice your way to becoming a good golfer—if you understand your golf swing. And by the way: Spend most of that time mastering the driver, wedge and putter. Learn those clubs and you've got it made.

Set Some Goals

Golf is like anything else in life: You'll achieve more if you set goals and work toward them. When I first started playing golf as a teenager,

I was enthralled by the Curtis Cup competition. I decided then and there that I wanted to play in one. From that point, every practice ball I hit, every round I played, every lesson I took, was geared toward helping me achieve that goal. Fortunately, I made the team twice. You can do the same thing. Set a goal to shave five or ten strokes off your handicap; to break eighty at your home course; to qualify for the championship flight. You'll become a better player by *defining* what you want to accomplish. Every year, many of the ladies who return to my Golfaris are so excited when they have improved their handicap that year to go into a more advanced group. I have some ladies who have come as beginners and are now in the advanced group.

Putting Simplified

Some people make putting too complicated. The best putters are the ones with the simplest strokes, with the fewest moving parts, with the fewest mental reminders flowing through their heads. Work to develop a stroke that uses the shoulders and arms to move the putter back and through. Never break the wrists. My thoughts over the ball are always, "Low, slow, accelerate." This prevents me from picking the putter up and jabbing at the ball. It's very important not to "quit" on the putt or decelerate through impact.

The Eye Drop Test

Sometimes a golfer will feel like he's making a good stroke on the greens, but nothing will fall into the hole. Often this is a result of poor aiming, which is caused by poor head position at address. Try this: Assume address position and hold a golf ball between your eyes. Now drop it. If your eyes are positioned directly above your ball, the dropped ball will hit the one on the green. If it misses, adjust your head position until you get it right. The putts will start to fall.

Spot Every Shot

Aiming every shot in golf, from a three-foot putt to a drive, is much easier with the age-old practice of "spotting" the ball. This is an important technique for all beginners to ingrain into their games. In lining up a putt, pick a spot on your target line five to eight inches in front of the ball. Then set the blade of the putter so your ball will roll over that spot. Do the same thing with chips and pitches. With full shots, you might pick a spot about three feet in front of your ball. This will help you pinpoint your aim a little better on longer shots.

Make Putting Fun

Practicing putting can be very boring if you don't enliven it with some sort of "game." Here are a couple that will help on long putts and short putts.

Speed is the key on approach putts of twenty to thirty feet. Most three-putts result from leaving these putts way short or hitting them too hard. Take a piece of chalk and draw a circle three feet in diameter around a cup on the practice green. Don't worry about making putts; just try to get inside the "peach basket."

A good drill for those crucial short putts is to put tees in the ground one foot from the cup, two feet, three feet, and so on. Then make five consecutive putts from the first tee, then from the second, and on back to five feet. If you miss a putt, start all over again.

A variation on this drill is putting around the cup in a circle. Putt three-footers around the cup and don't quit until you make every one. These drills will develop consistency under pressure.

A word of caution about putting practice: It can be hard on your back. I always straighten up between every putt and pause briefly. It's too much stress on your back to stay crouched over in your putting stance for too long.

Distance The Key In Short Game

The quickest way to lowering your score is to master distances from one hundred yards and in. Most pitch and chip shots that don't get near the hole are hit too soft or too firm. Nearly all three-putts result from first putts that are left short of the hole or roll way past.

A helpful rule in measuring distances on chip shots is to start with a seven-iron and recognize that, on a relatively flat area, a seven-iron chip will fly in the air about one-third of the total distance of the shot and then roll two-thirds. A five-iron, then, will roll a little more, a nine- iron a little less. An invaluable hour of practice time can be spent around a green, stepping off chip shots of various lengths with various clubs. Use tees stuck in the green as targets for landing the ball, then watch and see how far each chip shot rolls. The next time you play, you'll have a much better feel for distance on your chip shots.

Think Left To Chip Right

The majority of golfers I've taught over the years share one common fault: They're haunted by an assortment of fat and bladed shots from around the green that prevent them from getting "up and down" and turning bogeys into pars. Most of them benefit by emphasizing

GOLF WORLD 35¢

NEWSWEEKLY™ June 6, 1972

Titleholders Renewed

Sponsors Warren and Peggy Kirk Bell flank winner
Sandra Palmer to bestow green coat, and new crown
trophy, following 10-shot victory in renewal of the
Titleholders at Pine Needles. Page 6.

Peggy and Warren Bell are pictured on the cover of "Golf World" magazine in
June, 1972, crowing Sandra Palmer as the champion of the Titleholders, held that
year at Pine Needles. Peggy won the tournament as an amateur, and she and
Bullet hosted the event more than twenty years later. Palmer was the only golfer
in the field to break par for seventy-two holes, scoring a one-under total of 283.

the left side in chipping. Address the ball with an open stance, most of your weight on your left side, the ball centered and your hands slightly ahead of the ball. Then let the left hand and arm power the stroke back and through the ball. By keeping the right hand quiet, you avoid trying to scoop the ball.

Use The "T-T-T" For Better Chipping

We've helped many golfers through the years chip better by using the "Triangle, Track and Target" drill. You begin by placing two clubs on the ground on either side of the ball, about six inches apart. This is your track. Address the ball as I described above, and think of the triangle formed by your two arms and an imaginary line connecting your shoulder blades. As you hit the shot, keep the clubhead in the track and never let the triangle break down. Finally, make sure the back of your left hand is extended toward the target at follow through. Try this for thirty minutes one day, hitting shot after shot and concentrating on keeping the triangle intact, the clubhead on track and the back of the left hand extended to the target on the follow through.

The Grip: The Game's Bedrock

I will spend one lesson, two lessons, however many are necessary correcting a poor grip, especially with ladies. Men can sometimes get away with a poor grip because their strength allows them to make a solid hit anyway. (That doesn't mean, however, that men can't benefit from a better grip.) But not women. If your hands are out of position, you'll never improve as much as you'd like.

I use the traditional Vardon grip, with the little finger of the right hand overlapping the forefinger of the left. This grip makes the two hands feel and work as one. The Vs formed by both thumbs and forefingers should point between the neck and the right shoulder.

A couple of subtle points about the grip that I favor are, one, having a "short thumb" on the left hand and, two, having a "trigger finger" on the right hand. The short thumb means placing the left thumb relatively high on the shaft, rather than stretching it too far down the shaft, under the right hand. I think this provides more stability in the swing. I stretch my right forefinger just a fraction of an inch down the shaft, leaving a little space between it and my middle finger. This gives me more power and more control through the hitting zone.

The Little Circle Waggle

I used to spend a lot of time in the winter playing tournament golf, and between tournaments Babe Zaharias and I often visited Tommy Armour in Boca Raton. We'd have lessons in the morning and then tee it up in the afternoon. Tommy's first lesson with me was to teach me to waggle. He showed me how he made small, half circles—taking the club back straight down the target line, then back down inside the line, just as the swing itself should be. "It's the swing in miniature," he said. To this day I still use the little circle waggle.

But no matter what kind of waggle you develop, it's important to keep some part moving as you stand over the ball. If you're completely still, you can lock up and never pull the trigger. You might move your feet a little; you might move your head to take one last look at the target. It's like dancing. There's a rhythmic flow to everything.

Turn and Return

It's helpful to develop better body movement through the golf swing by thinking of "turn and return." You turn away from the target on the backswing, using a good shoulder turn. Then you return through the hitting area, pointing your belt buckle at the target on the follow through. While you've turned the upper body and hips on the backswing, you initiate the downswing with the lower body, using the feet, knees and hips. Sam Snead used to say he started his downswing by moving his left knee toward the target. Jack Nicklaus says he pushes off on the right leg. The point, though, is the same—you start the downswing by driving the legs and knees and moving the left hip out of the way.

Keep The Post

Ninety percent of the golfers I've taught are afflicted with one major problem—they sway their hips to the right on the backswing (for a right-handed golfer). This kills, from the beginning, any chance of making a powerful swing. Swaying causes the shoulders to dip downward and away from the target, and since they're out of position on the downswing, the release is very arms-and-hands oriented, and the weight ends up on the back leg at impact.

The solution to this is to "keep the post" on the backswing. The right leg must feel as if it's staying in the same position, with almost the same knee flex, throughout the swing. The weight should go on the inside of the right heel on the backswing. This turning the right hip around the post will provide a solid right side and will help you drive through the ball on the follow through.

Babe Zaharias (R) first invited Peggy to be her partner in the Hollywood Four-Ball in 1947: "I need a partner and you need to win."

Left Heel Stays Down

Not everyone in golf agrees with me on the proper position of the left heel at the top of the backswing. Jack Nicklaus has won twenty major championships by lifting his heel, so that's something in itself. Babe Zaharias had a short backswing, and her left heel also came up, but her first move on the downswing was with the left heel. The first time I played golf with Glenna Collett Vare, I noticed how quickly she lifted her left heel and then slapped it back down. "That's her secret," I said excitedly to myself, and started copying her. Helen Sigel Wilson, who playing with us, asked me what on earth I was doing. "I'm trying to copy Glenna's foot action," I said. Helen responded: "That popping up and down is probably the worst part of Glenna's swing."

Since then, I've decided that such movement is okay for the truly gifted players. My left heel comes up a fraction. But for the average player, lifting the left heel too high can only create problems. It can lead to swaying and to stiffening the right leg, which prevents moving through the ball.

Swing The Club, Don't Hit The Ball

It's sad but true: Many of the best swings on a golf course are practice swings. How many times have you been on the course with a caddie, and you make a practice swing and he says, "That's it, nice and smooth," and then you dump your ball in a bunker? Too many, probably. What happens is we're relaxed and loose when there's no ball in the way. We swing the club. But then we step up to the ball, and now we've got to hit the ball and we tense up. Think of swinging the club to the target; forget about hitting the ball. If you make a smooth swing, the ball just gets in the way and goes where you're aiming.

Tee Off from the Trouble Side

A good way to avoid trouble off the tee is to tee off from the side of trouble. If there's a lake left of the fairway, tee off from the left of the tee box. If there's a menacing bunker on the right, hit from the right side. By teeing off from the side of trouble, you'll automatically aim away from the trouble just by trying to hit the middle of the fairway.

Have Positive Thoughts

A corollary to the previous dictum is to concentrate on where you want to go, don't worry about where you don't want to go. For example, say you're playing a par-four, dogleg right, with a pond at the corner of the dogleg. Tee your ball on the right side of the tee, so you'll aim away from the pond. Then visualize your ball flying high against the blue sky and falling in the center to left-center of the fairway. Don't even think about the pond. If there's a deep bunker fronting a green, visualize your shot landing on the green; don't think of it falling into the bunker. You'll be surprised how this practice can keep you loose and confident and help prevent the bad swings that always seem to guide the ball into trouble.

Feel the Right Elbow

The right elbow plays an important role in the proper release of the club. If it's out of position on the downswing, it's difficult to get the club in the proper position to make a powerful pass at the ball. Thinking of keeping your elbows together throughout the swing helps some players. Feel like you're almost brushing your right hip with your right elbow through the hitting zone. This allows your forearms to rotate and your hands to turn over, which is the release that provides clubhead speed and power.

A word of warning, though. Some golfers take this concept too far and restrict the right elbow too close to their bodies at address. This causes many problems, such as fanning the club on the backswing and restricting a wide arc on the backswing.

There's an excellent training aid available in most golf shops and equipment catalogs that straps your arms and elbows into the proper position throughout the golf swing. I recommend it highly.

Kids Golf: Grip And Fun

There are only two things about teaching a child to play golf that are important. One, get his or her grip right from the beginning. Two, let them have fun.

There are exceptions, of course, but generally speaking, you can't play good golf unless you have a good grip. And changing a bad one after years of getting accustomed to a bad one is very, very difficult. So if you're going to introduce a child to golf, get his grip right from the beginning.

Beyond that, just let them have fun. It's fine to teach them the fundamentals—such as posture and swing path—but don't get hung up on beating balls and learning swing techniques. Kids will make a natural swing at the ball that will surprise you. They're great mimics. Show them a swing and say, "Copy that." Give them a good grip and let them fall in love with golf on their own. Then you've got a lifetime to teach them technique. ∎

Annika Sorenstam is all smiles following her dominating victory in the 1996 U.S. Women's Open at Pine Needles—back-to-back titles coupled with her win the previous year at The Broadmoor.

CHAPTER SEVEN

A NEW CENTURY

S pectators to the third round of the 2007 U.S. Women's Open at Pine Needles were lined up fifteen deep in the merchandise pavilion, waiting for Peggy Kirk Bell to sign copies of her book, *The Gift of Golf*. The "Grande Dame" of North Carolina golf inscribed and chatted, inscribed and smiled, inscribed and reminisced while soaking in the atmosphere of big-time golf at her family-owned and operated resort.

"Thanks, Peggy, for what you've done for golf and women's golf especially," one woman said.

Peggy accepted the compliment graciously but shrugged off the notion she's done anything special.

"For us to have had three Opens on a golf course we bought that had nothing but weeds and scrub oaks right up to the fairway is an amazing story," she says of her 1953 purchase of the course along with newlywed husband Warren (a.k.a "Bullet"). "My husband and I both loved the game and we both wanted to own our own business. All I've done is play a wonderful game. Everything I have in life has been through golf. It's been a joy and a blessing."

The modern evolution of the Pine Needles and Mid Pines stories has included the 1994 marriage of the two exemplary resorts on either side of Midland Road just west of Southern Pines; the successful production of three Women's Opens at Pine Needles in 1996, 2001 and '07; a loving and meticulous restoration of the Pine Needles golf course in 2004; overhauls and upgrades of the sleeping, dining and gathering rooms at both properties; and expansion of the practice and teaching facilities that have kept Pine Needles and its nationally renowned "Golfari" women's golf schools at the cutting edge of golf instruction.

"The way it all fell into place, all I believe is that it was all God's plan," Peggy says.

***

Championship golf actually had a brief flirtation with Pine Needles and the Bell family as long ago as 1967. Joe Dey, executive director of the United States Golf Association, wrote to the Bells asking if they'd like to host the U.S. Women's Open two years hence in 1969.

"The problem was that we had to put up a $20,000 purse," Peggy says. "Bullet and I wanted to do it, but we didn't think we could afford it. At the time, we were in debt building Pine Needles, so we didn't pursue it."

Peggy always had a soft spot in her heart for the Titleholders Championship, an event that ranked as one of the top competitions for lady golfers in the mid-twentieth century. It was held each spring at Augusta Country Club and served as the ladies' equivalent of the Masters. Peggy won the tournament as an amateur in 1949, and after it was discontinued in 1966, the Bells revived it for one year in 1972 and moved it to Pine Needles. In tribute to the Titleholders' long-held logo, Bullet commissioned the forging of a forty-inch, 266-pound crown made of bronze and had it mounted on a wood frame over a brick-based wishing well in front of the lodge entrance. He also had eight-inch replicas of the crown produced for the Titleholders' former champions and its new winner, who turned out to be Sandra Palmer with a 283 total. The tournament lost money for the resort and the Titleholders' Southern Pines fling lasted only one year. But the crown remains today.

"It cost us thirty-six hundred dollars to have those crowns made, which was more than Sandra earned for winning the tournament," Peggy says. "That shows you what purses were like for women's golf back then."

Peggy was long-time friends with two accomplished amateur golf-

THOMAS TOOHEY BROWN

Sorenstam (L) was at the top of women's golf in 1996 while Karrie Webb was equally imperious in outdistancing the 2001 Women's Open field.

ers and USGA committee members who had made their way up the USGA hierarchy as the 1980s evolved. Barbara McIntire followed Peggy at Rollins College and as a Curtis Cup team member and was a six-time champion of the Women's North and South Amateur at Pinehurst. Judy Bell (no relation) was another top amateur in the mid-1900s and developed an expertise in rules and course set-up; in 1987 she became the first woman to serve on the USGA Executive Committee. Those women recognized Peggy's contributions to the game of golf and Pine Needles' excellence as a potential championship venue and were instrumental in Pine Needles being selected as site of the 1989 U.S. Girls Junior (won by Brandie Burton) and the 1991 Women's Senior Amateur (won by Phyllis Preuss).

At the opening night dinner for the Senior Amateur, Peggy addressed the competitors and officials and said, "Well, we've had the senior ladies and we've had the young girls. Now if we could get the pros in here, we'd have it covered."

Judy Bell approached Peggy afterward and asked, "Would you like to have a U.S. Open here?"

"Are you kidding?" Peggy responded.

"We'll work on it," Judy said.

By the time the PGA Tour came to Pinehurst No. 2 for the 1991 Tour Championship in late October, the deal was struck: Pine Needles would be the site of the 1996 U.S. Women's Open.

"Pine Needles is a place you should have a U.S. Open at," said LPGA Hall of Famer Kathy Whitworth. "It's a perfect venue. With the history of the area, the tradition, the quality of the golf course, it lends itself to an Open. This is the kind of place you expect to come for a U.S. Open."

"Pine Needles is a classic Donald Ross design," added Kendra Graham, USGA director of women's competitions. "People in the golf world know about Pine Needles. It's a hidden gem."

No one knew exactly what to expect when the USGA ventured to Southern Pines in 1996 for the Women's Open. But all questions were answered with aplomb: Only two players broke par for seventy-two holes, with Annika Sorenstam winning in a six-shot rout with a 272 total, eight-under; an Open record at the time of 106,000 attendees converged on the Pine Needles campus; and parking, traffic flow and accommodations were manageable and sufficient.

Sorenstam's triumph was apropos given her ties to Peggy Bell forged several years earlier. Sorenstam grew up in Stockholm but moved to the United States for college, playing at the University of Arizona in the early 1990s. She made the acquaintance at a tournament in Palm Springs of longtime University of Washington women's golf coach Edean Ihlanfeldt, who had been friends for many years with Peggy. One year Ihlanfeldt called Bell and asked if a young Swedish golfer could stay with Peggy while competing in the North and South Women's Amateur at Pinehurst. Bell said Sorenstam was welcome, and thus the extroverted Bell and introverted Sorenstam began a close friendship.

"I gave her a car, a room and told her to come and go as she pleased," Peggy remembers. "She was quiet as a mouse. We had golf schools that week, so I was never able to go see her play, but they said she hit it long and straight. I know she was disappointed when she lost."

Sorenstam finished at Arizona in 1992, began playing the LPGA Tour in 1993 and was Rookie of the Year the following season. In June 1995, she broke into the national spotlight by winning the Women's Open at The Broadmoor Golf Club in Colorado Springs. Among the spectators that week were Peggy Bell and a party from Pine Needles, the site of the Open the next year.

"I hugged Annika after she won and said, 'Now you can win it again at Pine Needles!'" Peggy says.

Sorenstam did exactly that.

"Winning at Pine Needles is very special to me," Sorenstam said after the win. "I will never forget Peggy Bell and Pine Needles."

The week flowed so smoothly and the golf course proved such an excellent test that the USGA accepted the Bells' invitation to return for another Open. That 2001 engagement was announced before the last player had departed Pine Needles on Sunday afternoon.

"We decided it would be a good idea to come back here," Judy Bell said. "This family and this community are passionate about golf. There is such a feeling for the game here. The people of this community and state embraced the event. That's a key with us."

Throughout the week, Peggy could hardly move through the crowds without being besieged by autograph-seekers and old friends and acquaintances. It delighted her to see each of her children and their spouses involved in the operation of the championship. Volunteers, sponsors, patrons and contestants marveled that, despite the size of the event, the same family atmosphere that had prevailed since the early 1950s was alive and well.

Next to Peggy, perhaps the championship's other key figure was

Golf fans flocked by the thousands to Pine Needles for its three U.S. Women's Opens in 1996, 2001 and 2007, with the practice range providing one of the most popular viewing spots. Cristie Kerr (inset) collected her first major championship by topping the field by two shots in 2007.

PINE NEEDLES LODGE & GOLF CLUB

her late husband, Bullet, who died in 1984. She and her children never forgot the influence he had in building the resort and its reputation in the early days.

"All of this is possible because of Bullet," Peg said.

"I can't help thinking that Dad's up there saying, 'You did all right, kids,'" added eldest daughter Bonnie.

Five years later, Karrie Webb posted a 273 total and won by eight shots. This time, approximately 100,000 fans attended (despite rain-outs on Monday and Friday) and the next Open for 2007 had been awarded to Pine Needles by the time the last putt had dropped.

"We had one of the better championships in 1996 and here we are five years later with an even better experience," said Graham. "They have raised the bar as far as everything that goes into hosting a championship."

The course was hailed for its intrigue and old-world charm during the 1996 and 2001 Women's Opens. Set at a par seventy with one par-five on each side, the course yielded low scores to the respective winners—Sorenstam at eight-under and Webb at seven-under. Only one other player in those two events broke par, that being Kris Tschetter's 278 total in '96.

"What's remarkable is the two best players at the time won, and they won by a lot," noted Pat McGowan, Bonnie's husband and a former PGA Tour player. "What that showed us, and it's a real compliment, is the course was very difficult, but if you get the best player in the world on fire, you can still shoot amazing scores. It can be done, but you'd really better be right on."

One golfer quietly developing an affinity for Pine Needles and maturing as her golf career evolved during those two Women's Opens was Cristie Kerr. The Miami native took low amateur honors as an eighteen-year-old in '96 and tied for fourth in '01 during her fifth year on the LPGA Tour. By late June of 2007, when the curtain lifted on the third installment of the Pine Needles-Women's Open chapter, Kerr had collected nine tournament victories but was tagged with a "best player yet to win a major" albatross. Now twenty-nine, newly married and having learned to manage her prodigious length, deft putting stroke and fiery emotions, Kerr found a soothing karma in the Sandhills.

"When I stepped on the grounds this week, it was just magic," she said. "Some things are just meant to happen."

Kerr drilled an eighteen-foot birdie putt on the fourteenth hole in the final round to take the lead from Lorena Ochoa, the top-ranked player in the world, and then held on during the homestretch to post a final-round seventy, a total of 279 and a two-shot win over Ochoa and eighteen-year-old Angela Park.

"We have never seen her this at ease," caddie Jason Gilroyed said. "She loves it here. Last year she said, 'If I am going to win my first major, it's going to be at Pine Needles.'"

"I'm going to give this trophy a very, very special place in my house," Kerr said. "I might even build some lights and stuff around it."

The golf course the 2007 field encountered still had the timeless soft lines, the strategic nuances and the ebb and flow of a fine old Ross layout. But this course was new in the respect that the greens, tees and bunkers had all been replaced during a 2004 restoration. The Bell family planned in 2002 to reconstruct the greens prior to the '07 Open, but resort President and CEO Kelly Miller and course superintendent Dave Fruchte came across several pieces of memorabilia that prompted them to make the project more wide-sweeping.

Fruchte found a series of aerial photographs of the course from the North Carolina Division of Soil & Water Conservation. The photos, taken in 1939, 1950 and 1966, showed that the size and shapes of greens and the positioning of tees, bunkers and fairway boundaries had changed over the years. In addition, tree growth over the decades had confined some hole dimensions and limited the supply of sunlight and air to some greens complexes.

Fruchte scanned the photos and enlarged them on his computer. He, Miller and McGowan studied each hole for nuances that had been lost.

"Over the years the greens became smaller and more oval-shaped," Miller said. "Originally they were much larger and quite varied in shape."

"They flattened out and lost some of their character," McGowan added.

Then Miller visited the Tufts Archives in Pinehurst and found an old scorecard for the course and an article about Pine Needles from an old issue of *The Pinehurst Outlook*. He noted that No. 14 was originally a par-four and was now a par-five, and No. 15 was originally a par-five and was now a par-four.

"At some point there was a house built behind the fifteenth tee that made them move the tees up," Miller said. "I guess that's when it became a four and they made new tees for fourteen and made it a five."

DONALD J. ROSS
GOLF ARCHITECT

Pine Needles Lodge & Golf Club   No. **14** GREEN

PINES

1. Maintain original green.

2. Restore greenside bunkering to original design.

3. Restore back collar to original design.

Restoration by:
John Fought

The 2004 Pine Needles restoration project was coordinated by architect John Fought and included turning the 14th hole back into its original configuration as a par-four.

CHIP HENDERSON

Miller and McGowan consulted with John Fought, a former collegiate teammate of McGowan's at Brigham Young University in the 1970s, later a tour pro and by the late 1980s a full-time golf course architect. Fought began his design career on the staff of Bob Cupp, and in doing so traveled the country and studied the heirlooms of the Eastern golf establishment, among them Shinnecock Hills, Winged Foot, Quaker Ridge and the National Golf Links. He devoured the volumes on classic architecture in golf's extensive library. He was Cupp's lead designer in the creation of Pumpkin Ridge, a thirty-six hole complex in Oregon that drew widespread critical acclaim upon its opening in 1992.

"Much of my interest in architecture evolved during my playing career," Fought said. "That's when we were playing TPC courses that looked like they were on the moon. Pumpkin Ridge was a throwback. It was designed in the classic motif. The lines are subtle, the grades are long, the slopes tie in beautifully and naturally."

Fought was hired to coordinate the restoration—a project that began as a simple greens rebuilding and morphed into something far more significant.

The greens foundations were rebuilt to USGA specifications for proper drainage and the surfaces re-sprigged with Penn A-1 bentgrass to provide a smooth roll of the ball and the faster speeds preferred today.

The pars on the fourteenth and fifteenth holes were reversed to their original configurations. New tees on twelve holes stretched the championship-tee length to the 7,000-yard neighborhood, and a new green extended the short par-five tenth by sixty-five yards. With the added length, golfers were now required to hit some of the same shots demanded eighty years ago before the advent of white-hot balls and titanium drivers. Ross's original design called for tee shots to land on the faces of fairway slopes and come quickly to rest on the crest of an upslope. Modern technology had allowed good golfers to crack their drives over the hills and within pitching wedge range of the green on long par-fours.

"One of our goals was to rediscover the golf course," Fought said.

"We wanted to remind people that this is a Donald Ross golf course and will remain a Donald Ross golf course. We're trying to get back to Ross in everything we can. Some elements have been lost. We're stepping back in time and rediscovering some of the things he did."

What Fought was looking for was a fashion that could work in the

Roaring Twenties and one that's aesthetically pleasing and strategically appealing in the twenty-first century.

"The course is being rapidly moulded into a project of beauty that will satisfy both the eye of the artist and the exacting demands of golfers familiar with the preeminent links of America and Europe," *The Pinehurst Outlook* noted during the course's construction in 1927.

Some eighty years later, Fought stood with Miller and McGowan as they watched a bulldozer tear up the tenth green in the early stages of the restoration.

"I'd say we're committed now," Fought said. "No turning back."

Throughout the duration of the project, more than two years from research and planning to construction and grow-in, Fought carried the weight of history.

"I felt like the ghost of Ross was with me," he says. "That's a powerful thing."

As the second decade of twenty-first century ensued, Pine Needles and Mid Pines drew yet another link to their roots. Both were originally conceived as private clubs—with the golf courses and amenities open only to members or hotel guests. But after the bankruptcies by original ownership groups in the 1930s and scuttling of the properties through various owners until landing in stable hands in the 1950s, both clubs have essentially operated as resorts—open to overnight guests with tee times available to outside play on an as-available basis.

Miller announced in the spring of 2010 a membership program that sought to connect the two courses more to the Southern Pines-Pinehurst community. For a quite reasonable initiation fee and monthly dues, members gained access to at least one of the Ross-designed courses on a daily basis. Local and out-of-town memberships are available.

"Our industry has changed dramatically through the recent recession and economic turmoil," Miller said in April 2010. "The *game* of golf is still very healthy. The *industry* of golf has problems. People who love the game are still playing. Making these two great courses available under one membership addresses that core golfer. They can't do any better than Mid Pines and Pine Needles. In that sense, we've returned to our roots." ∎

Afterword

By James Dodson

O ut of the blue following church one warm spring Sunday after-noon in1966, my dad suggested I fetch my golf clubs and come along with him. I'd been sulking around the house since the previous afternoon when the old pro at his club in Greensboro, a profane living legend named Aubrey Apple, booted me off the golf course for the unspeakable crime of losing my 13-year-old temper and burying my Bulls Eye putter to the hilt in the 14th green after missing a short birdie putt. I was playing with my dad and a pair of his regular playing partners at the time—the first time I'd been allowed to take my game to a regulation golf course.

Banished from the course until further notice by Pro, fearing an entire summer might pass before I would be allowed back, I was only too happy to fetch my clubs and see where he might take us. We wound up mysteri-ously driving down a pine-girdled road to the Sandhills, to a place I'd only heard others speak about.

We passed a beautiful hotel and golf course where caddies were assist-ing players and my dad casually remarked, "That's Pinehurst No. 2, a very famous golf course."

I brightened considerably. "Are we going to play there?"

"Nope," he said, and fell maddeningly silent. We rode further down pretty Midland Road and suddenly turned into the grounds of another beautiful hotel sitting serenely in the pines.

"What's this place?" I asked.

"It's called the Mid Pines Hotel. I have a friend who wants to meet you."

We parked and followed a path that led us around the corner of the building to a gorgeous fairway framed by dogwoods in bloom.

In the pro shop, my dad introduced me to his friend, Ernie Bo-ros, the head professional. The name instantly meant something to me. The U.S. Open of 1963 was perhaps the first golf telecast I ever watched, won by Julius Boros. "Are you related to him?" I asked this

PINE NEEDLES LODGE & GOLF CLUB

Pine Needles and Mid Pines both offer an idyllic setting for golfers—newcomers to the game as well as seasoned professionals.

Mr. Boros.

"Sure am," he replied. "Julie's my brother. Would you like to meet him? I think he's around here somewhere."

I was speechless. A few minutes later, two-time U.S. Open winner Julius Boros came out from the hotel dining room. We shook hands and he asked me if I liked golf. I told him I loved golf. He asked me if I respected the game the way it deserved to be respected. I assured him that I did—although I didn't dare make eye contact with my old man.

"Good," he said. "Smart players never throw their clubs. Do you throw clubs?"

"Well," I was forced to admit, "sometimes. But not much."

He nodded. "Well," he said gently. "Let's cut that out from now on, okay?"

I promised him I would never throw a club again and saw him reach for a white visor with the distinctive Mid Pines crest on it. "Would you like me to sign this?" he asked. I said yes and thanked him. Boros offered me his hand, smiled his lazy catfish smile, and told me not to forget my promise to behave. Then he went back to his afternoon lunch.

"Wasn't that something?" my dad said after we walked outside to have a look at the 18th green of the golf course where, as I recall, a group was just finishing their round. No golf course had ever looked more inviting to me, more serene and perfect.

"I hope you keep your promise to Mr. Boros," he remarked.

The view of the 1922 Mid Pines Inn as seen from the eighteenth fairway ranks with the great sights in golf anywhere.

I assured him I would. He thought for a moment and then said, "In that case, let's get our clubs and play."

That afternoon stays with me almost like no other because Mid Pines became the first regulation golf course I ever played. That alone makes it magical and unique, yet every time I returned over subsequent decades — through my teenage years and college days, and then on into a working journalism career — my admiration for the Donald Ross course, the venerable hotel, the sedate beauty and grandeur of Mid Pines itself, only grew and deepened. In due course, I came to have similar almost custodial feelings about Peggy Kirk Bell's beautiful Pine Needles Resort and the Ross gem of a golf course there.

Because of a most fortunate golf writing career that has taken me around the world and allowed me to play many of the game's most celebrated layouts, I'm often asked if I have a favorite place to play. My reply never varies.

"If I could only play one golf course for the rest of my life, it would probably be Mid Pines," I'll reply with a qualifying grin of a second-chance kid. "Then again, it might be Pine Needles."

For the record, I lost that treasured Boros visor years ago. But I never threw a club or buried a putter in a green again — at least when my old man was anywhere around. ∎

James Dodson is a best-selling author who lives in Southern Pines; he edits "PineStraw" magazine and writes a Sunday essay for "The Pilot."

CHAPTER EIGHT

PHOTO ALBUM

PINE NEEDLES LODGE & GOLF CLUB

A gallery follows the action during a mid-20th century tournament at the Pine Needles fourth hole (current third). Donald Ross (R), the designer of the golf courses at Pine Needles and Mid Pines, used a sand-clay base for the original greens before the development and introduction of grass greens to the Sandhills area in the mid-1930s.

PINE NEEDLES LODGE & GOLF CLUB

A contrast in eras: the 10th hole at Pine Needles (left) and two greens from today, the 14th at Mid Pines (top) and the 18th at Pine Needles. In the early days, only the fairways, greens and tees were maintained; otherwise, the roughs were sand and wire grass.

145

The second hole at Mid Pines is one of the most picturesque and challenging on the golf course—the par-3 requires a shot of about 170 yards to a shallow green heavily guarded by bunkers.

CHIP HENDERSON

The holes at Mid Pines, like the par-five 15th, are framed by mature pines and hardwoods, pine straw forests and flowering shrubs. Gently angled fairways require precise aim off the tee and small greens place a premium on accuracy with the irons.

MID PINES CARD

1	4	379	10	5	514
2	3	178	11	3	174
3	4	414	12	4	380
4	4	330	13	3	230
5	5	470	14	4	361
6	5	500	15	5	481
7	4	383	16	4	400
8	3	179	17	4	391
9	4	340	18	4	411

TOTAL PAR 72, YARDS 6,515

CHIP HENDERSON

The entry side of Mid Pines Inn at night. The building was opened in 1922 and designed in the Georgian style, with white columns and half-brick, half-wood siding exteriors.

MID PINES INN & GOLF CLUB

The third hole at Pine Needles requires a short-iron tee shot of only 120 yards, but the narrow green slopes from back-to-front and is tightly guarded on either side by bunkers.

CHIP HENDERSON

From the green looking back toward the tee on the uphill par-four fourth at Pine Needles.

CHIP HENDERSON

Pine Needles Card

1	5	482	10	5	482
2	4	438	11	4	369
3	3	135	12	4	350
4	4	382	13	3	181
5	3	181	14	4	402
6	4	411	15	5	485
7	4	407	16	3	169
8	4	353	17	4	432
9	4	371	18	4	406

TOTAL PAR 71, YARDS 6,436

The long, wispy grasses bordering the par-three 13th hole at Pine Needles give this area of the back nine a look and feel of the windswept British Isles.

CHIP HENDERSON

The clubhouse and practice putting green rest serenely at dusk after another day of golf, competition and companionship at Pine Needles.

CHIP HENDERSON

The azaleas blooming during the springtime add to the ambiance of the 12th hole at Mid Pines.